This book is due for return on or before the last date shown below.

7 JUL 2005

1 0 DEC 2005

Don Gresswell Ltd., London, N.21   Cat. No. 1208

DG 02242/71

# MARIA FAY'S
# FLOOR BARRE

# MARIA FAY'S
# FLOOR BARRE

**Demonstrated by Christina Beskou**
**Drawings by Josephine Jewkes**
**Photographs by Angela Taylor**

First published in 2003 by Dance Books Ltd, 4 Lenten Street, Alton, Hampshire GU 34 1HG

Printed in Great Britain by H. Charlesworth & Co., Huddersfield

ISBN: 1 85273 089 7

# CONTENTS

# ACKNOWLEDGEMENTS

I would like to thank all the dancers, professional students, critics, colleagues, friends, my husband and family who encouraged me to write and publish the floor barre system that I created and taught during the last four decades of my teaching career.

I particularly wish to thank Christina Beskou and Tim Almas for being such indefatigable and outstanding demonstrators when modelling for the photographs and drawings; Angela Taylor for working with us so unselfishly and skifully on making those many artistic photographs and Josephine Jewkes for her patience and devotion while creating her drawings.

Special thanks to Mary Clark who published continuously for two years a great part of the exercises of my floor barre system in *The Dancing Times*; David Leonard from Dance Books Publishers for recognising the need and interest of the dancing profession for a textbook of this specific system and Liz Morrell and Patrick Donnelly who designed this book with so much expertise and interest.

I am much indebted to Charles Hedges who—as always—generously helped me in correcting my inefficient grammar throughout the text.

Maria Fay
January 2003, Highgate

# THE AUTHOR AND THE CONTRIBUTORS

**Maria Fay** was born in Hungary where she was trained in classical ballet, character and contemporary dance from the age of six by Turnay, Kállai, Bercik, Nádasi, Messerer, Vainonen, Zakarov and Armachevskaja. After graduation she danced in several companies and became a leading dancer, and later choreographer, in the Budapest State Theatre. In 1956 together with her scientist husband she fled from Hungary and settled in England.

During the following years Maria taught and coached at professional level in her London studio as well as in 26 internationally-renowned ballet companies and 11 vocational schools all over the world (among them the Royal Ballet, the Royal Ballet Touring Company, the Royal Winnipeg Ballet, the Royal Swedish Ballet, the Royal Danish Ballet, the DutchNational Ballet, London Festival Ballet, the National Ballet of Spain, the National Ballet of China, Ballet Rambert, Grand Ballet du Marquis de Cuevas, Royal Ballet Upper and Lower School, the Royal Ballet School Teachers Training Course, the Royal Academy of Dancing Teachers Training Course, London School of Contemporary Dance).

She choreographed for Twentieth Century Fox, ITV and BBC television, the Royal Ballet, Covent Garden Opera Ballet, London Festival Ballet, Les Grands Ballets Canadien, the National Ballet of China.

She has given lectures in several universities, seminars, ballet clubs and dance organisations in the UK, North America, France and Austria.

Among her publications are several syllabi which were created for the Royal Academy of Dancing, two series of articles published over six years in *The Dancing Times*, two video tapes ('The Ballet Class' and 'Faults, Corrections and Perfections'), the book, *Mind Over Body* ( C.&A. Black). *Maria Fay's Floor Barre* is her latest publication, soon to have an accompanying video tape which will also be published by Dance Books.

One of the greatest joys she has is to watch and follow the progress of her many students who have become famous dancers, choreographers, teachers, directors of companies and vocational schools.

**Christina Beskou** received her classical and contemporary dance training from the age of 12 in Nelly Calvo's School Athens. She continued her studies in London at the Royal Academy of Dance Teachers Training Course from where she graduated with the advanced diploma level A.R.A.D. in 1976. Between 1979-81 she studied the Martha Graham technique at the London Contemporary School of Dance with Karen Bell Kanner. At the same time she had her regular ballet classes with Maria Fay and became her assistant and demonstrator. During this period she also learned Maria's Floor Barre and gained permission from her to teach it. Since then she has taught this system in Greece, England, Holland, Germany and Argentina. Christina danced with several dance companies in her own country and in other European countries. In 1989 she formed her own company, Seresta, of which she is the artistic director and choreographer. She performed with her ensemble in Greece, England, Holland, Luxemburg, France and Japan.

In 1998 Christina modelled for all the photographs used in Maria Fay's Floor Barre series in *The Dancing Times* and for this book. She is the dancer in the Floor Barre system on the forthcoming video tape.

**Josephine Jewkes** took her first dance lessons at home with her mother. Later she was educated at the Solihull School of Ballet, White Lodge and Bush Davies School, studying in the summer holidays with Cleo Nordi and Svetlana Beriosova. After joining London Festival Ballet at seventeen, Josephine began working privately with Maria Fay. This close relationship continued throughout her career as she rose to become Principal Dancer performing rôles such as Giselle/Myrtha (*Giselle*), Tatyana (*Onegin*), Odette (*Swan Lake*), Juliet (*Romeo and Juliet*), Prelude/Mazurka (*Les Sylphides*), Swanilda (*Coppèlia*), Sugar Plum Fairy (*Nutcracker*), Cinderella (*Cinderella*) and Aurora (*Sleeping Beauty*, guest tour). Maria Fay's Floor Barre became an essential method of rehabilitation after periods of rest or injury, as well as for warm-up and general conditioning.

In 1996 Josephine was invited to join Rambert Dance Company where she danced in works by Bruce, Kylian, Branstrup, Naharin, Cohan, Veldman and others. After retiring from dancing in 1999, Josphine graduated from Kingston University with a BA Hons. in Architecture. "I would like to express my love and gratitude to Maria Fay for those intense and unforgettable years."

**Angela Taylor** was a dancer trained at the Rambert School and later at Maria Fay's studio, from where she graduated. Having pursued a career in dance with companies abroad, including the National Ballet du Marseille and the Rome Ballet Theatre as well as at Covent Garden, she then studied photography specialising in dance and portraiture.

Commissions came from the Royal Ballet, Birmingham Royal Ballet, Rambert Dance Company, Ballet du Nord, Ballet de Monte Carlo, American Dance Theatre, Cuban National Ballet, the Kirov Ballet in St Petersburg and the Maurice Bejart company. She also works with trusts, organisations, workshop competitions and festivals including Royal Ballet Education, Gemini Trust Ethiopia, Christian Aid, F.I.T. in Havana and Cadiz and the Edinburgh Festival.

Her photographs appear in many national newspapers and in *Vogue*, *Opera*, *Dancing Times*, *Dance Magazine*, *Dance Europe*, *Ballet International* and *Dance* and in various books. She has shown her work in 24 exhibitions world-wide.

# PART I

# DEVELOPMENT OF A FLOOR BARRE

# DEVELOPMENT OF A FLOOR BARRE

## A System Based on and Complimenting a Classical Ballet Technique

In the early sixties I opened my own ballet studio in Philbeach Gardens London, where I taught open classes and coached many eminent dancers from both English and foreign ballet companies who wanted to take private lessons. Amongst these dancers was a young and exceptionally talented Australian, Barbara Croutain.

She was a protégé of Walter Gore and his ballerina wife, Paula Hinton, who was also working with me at that time. These two ladies practised hard and tirelessly to get into perfect shape for a new ballet ensemble which 'Wally' was planning to launch. Alas, for Barbara this was not to be. Shortly after rehearsals started she had an accident in which she injured her shin and knee. The leg needed an operation and to be put in a plaster cast.

A week after she returned from hospital I visited her. I found this otherwise cheerful and exceptionally lively girl in a deeply depressed state of mind. Understandably, an injury will upset any dancer but her situation was particularly sad. She knew that the newly-formed ensemble couldn't wait for her recovery which, at best, would take a minimum of three months, and that they would have to engage another dancer to replace her, immediately. In other words, she had missed the boat—and another one wasn't in sight! To add to all this misery, she had no financial support to keep herself going. She desperately needed some stimulation, reassurance and hope. I wanted to raise her spirits but it was obvious that verbal encouragement on its own would not do the trick. Dancers need action and this girl was deprived from it, and for some months.

I remembered only too well from my dancing years how I used to despair when I was ill or injured. I hated every minute of inactivity, feared the unavoidable loss of strength, stamina and suppleness and dreaded the thought of gaining excess weight. Instinctively, I wanted to find a way to keep my physique active, and at the same time, to rest the injured part of my body, instead of just feeling sorry for myself and waiting passively until I would be well again during what seemed an endless period of healing.

To keep up my spirits I devised for myself some gentle exercises that I could execute either lying on the floor or in bed. This was a quite unexpected solution for me as, ever since my student days when yoga and various other body-conditioning exercises were compulsory studies in our timetable, I had had a special dislike for them. (I considered them necessary but was inclined to turn up my nose as I thought them to be purely mechanical, dry, inartistic and boring!) However, in desperate times and as a last resort, I began to see them in a different light. What's more, being deprived of dancing, any kind of movement became a joy for me.

Depending on what my injury was, and trying to make sure that I didn't aggravate the troubled part of my body, practising these movements at least gave me the chance to work those muscles and joints which were unharmed. I tried to recall some of those exercises that I could execute in either a sitting position or while lying on a bed or the floor and which I trusted to strengthen, or loosen, stretch or relax, my uninjured muscles. Usually the greater part of a dancer's injury is connected with the lower limbs or the back. Therefore it seemed unwise that, while the injured parts of the body are healing, one should work in a vertical position, which by its very nature will force one to place the body weight on the affected leg. (Alas, classical dancers, when convalescing from illness or injury, often start their recovery with a 'gentle', upright barre exercise!)

Exercising myself during these healing periods proved to be beneficial from many points of view. My initial aim was to keep my physique in a comparatively mobile condition and in shape, but in keeping myself active I unintentionally avoided the typical depression from which most injured dancers suffer during periods of rehabilitation.

As I looked in Barbara's tearful face, and knowing how wretched her position was, it suddenly occurred to me that if I could recall some of my own 'exercises for invalids' and get her to practise them regularly, they might help her just as they had helped me.

To Barbara's great surprise, I said, "Instead of whining and moaning we had better start working on you, right now!"

"You must be joking," she answered, looking at her plaster cast. "How on earth can anyone do anything with this damned monster? It weighs a ton!" (At that time plaster casts were much heavier and clumsier than they are today.) For a minute, as I looked at this lifeless, stiff, long 'white tube', I felt that my own confidence also shrank. I had never had my leg and knee in a plaster cast so I wasn't sure whether my proposal was a feasible one but, wanting to help and having nothing better to offer, I thought I should conceal my doubts and give it a try. I pretended to be tough and 'unmoved' by her misery.

"What's all this fuss? After all, I am not asking you to work on a variation, simply to exercise a little, working just a little on your tummy, diaphragm, shoulders and back!" For a few seconds she looked at me as if I was totally out of my mind but, as she didn't have any choice in the matter, she 'surrendered' to my totalitarian attitude. Minutes later she was completely absorbed in executing some exercises on top of her bed. (Her rented room was so small that there was no floor space available to work on without endangering both her plastered leg and the few surrounding pieces of furniture.)

We were both amazed at how much we were able to achieve considering all the limitations we were up against. From then on, right through the following weeks, she needed no persuasion to practise every day. It was rewarding to see how she benefited physically from the limited programme of what she was capable of doing. In addition, her depression vanished.

However, the real trial was still to come when, five weeks later, the cast was removed. She was still in a state of shock when she hobbled on her crutches into my studio. "I will never be able to dance again," she whispered with a horror-stricken expression as she looked at her hardly recognizable leg, which had shrunk to the shape of a stick. In spite of being warned, when she first saw the muscle wastage of her misshapen leg and felt its weakness she couldn't believe the doctors' reassurance that this was just a normal phase in the healing procedure. She was convinced—as so many dancers are in similar circumstances—that the medical profession just doesn't quite understand yet how much strength and pliability is demanded of a dancer's sensitive and vulnerable muscle structure. I sensed that she needed encouragement and reassurance from someone who belonged to the dancing profession.

"You mustn't despair! It will take some time but your leg will regain its former strength and shape. Perhaps, with further floor exercises you will be able to shorten the usual recovery time without risking a relapse or further injury." As that was what she wanted to hear, I continued, "With the cast off, you will be able to carry out a much more sophisticated floor exercise programme. This will help you to regain your general strength and mobility much faster and then gradually you will be able to strengthen your injured leg, too. By the time your doctors allow you to start working in an upright position, your muscle structure will be pliable and relatively strong. You'll hardly need to struggle against the weakness, stiffness and associated symptoms from which dancers suffer when they let their bodies get out off condition during a healing period. A well-conditioned physique will help you to make a safe and speedy recovery."

With the help of a couple of sympathetic male dancers we cast aside her crutches, helped her sit on the studio floor, and started to exercise her.

I must confess that at the beginning I improvised a lot of Barbara's rehabilitation exercises. Although I had a great many of them at my disposal, I had neither a system of my own to follow nor one from somebody else.

I just used common sense when showing her a variety of exercises that I considered were suited to her present capabilities and, I suppose, I taught them to her in a sensible order. Frankly, my determination to help played a much greater part in my actions than the knowledge and experience I had in such matters at that time.

During the following weeks I carefully prepared her lessons. At the same time I was learning more about my 'new project' by constantly watching how her physique reacted to my programme and then making adjustments according to my observations. The result was rewarding and Barbara became fit sooner than anyone—including her doctors—expected. In addition, we both noticed that her breath control was far better and she was more pulled up and turned out than before.

Little did I know that this episode—which I looked on as a successful but rather insignificant experiment and deviation in my teaching career—has to become a prologue to a much longer experiment which occupied me during the next four decades of teaching and coaching!

*  *  *  *  *

At the time of Barbara's rehabilitation I had no intention of spending extra energy and time on further investigation or to think of it as a 'project' and create anything as ambitious as a system for dancers' rehabilitation or their conditioning.

However, before long, the word spread through the profession saying that I had 'special' exercises. Wherever I happened to be working as a ballet-mistress (whether in a company, vocational school or in my private studio) many dancers in various situations would ask me to help them using my remedial floor work.

The majority of these requests were mainly about rehabilitating the weakened physique of dancers after operations or typical dance injuries such as sprains, strains, shin-splints and the like. Although this kind of work has little to do with my artistic interests in teaching, curiously enough, instead of finding it boring (as I had in the past) I gradually found this 'side line' quite challenging. I enjoyed seeing the beneficial effects on the dancers and I was learning a lot through my teaching.

In the beginning I could base this project only on those early experiments I had made during my dancing years when I was my own guinea pig. Therefore these exercises were geared mainly to my own needs and physique. Now, teaching them to other dancers, I needed to observe and monitor how they affected differing physiques and gender—some may have been right for an average female dancer's muscle structure but didn't work for a generally more robust body of a male dancer—and adapt them accordingly to each given physique and circumstance.

The more experience I gained the more I realised that such a thing as a 'routine rehabilitation class' was out of the question even though there were numerous exercises designed for conditioning the body both partially and generally. Each dancer's problem, physique and healing process was different. They had to be dealt with individually. With each case I was learning something new, but sometimes I faced situations for which I was completely unprepared.

Jeremy Leslie Spinks was a graduate of mine who had just gained a contract with the Royal Norwegian Ballet —his first professional engagement. On the way to my studio he was the victim of a road accident. His ribs were fractured, a collarbone and a forearm as well as a thigh and shinbone were broken. In addition to these injuries his body was seriously bruised. When I visited him in hospital a couple of days afterwards I hardly recognised him as there was scarcely anything which wasn't covered in either bandages, ice packs or plaster of Paris—including his head and neck!

"Sorry, but it looks as though I won't be able to make class tomorrow," he mumbled while squinting with the one eye which was free of bandages.

"I can't see why? Aren't you a bit too finicky?" I tried to match his dry humour but could hardly control my tears. It was obvious that the fulfilment of his first contract was absolutely out of the question and I even feared that his career as a dancer was now in doubt.

"As a matter of fact... I wondered... as you are here anyway... would you mind very much teaching me some of your 'bed exercises'... please? I feel I could do something useful instead of just lazing here for who knows how long. All the physiotherapist could suggest was to wriggle my toes! I am sure there must be a lot more I could work on."

While I admired his courage and optimism I couldn't help having serious doubts. Never before have I been faced with such a case. I had little confidence as to his chance of recovering enough to be a dancer and I doubted my own capacity to help him. Could I create exercises that would suit his very limited powers without obstructing his healing process? I wanted to hide my fears from him and pretended to be cheerful and optimistic in order to keep up his spirits.

"OK, I'll try," (I heard myself saying) "but first we need your doctors' approval. In a few days I'll return and, if your doctors agree to the plan, I'll teach you some exercises." This gave me the necessary safeguard and a little time to prepare some 'made-to-measure' movements for him.

When we received the green light from the consultant we embarked on a very special programme. We patiently persevered for weeks, which ran into months. Because of what his shattered body would allow we progressed with the speed of a tortoise, from absolute minimum to a point where we could start dreaming about a return to ballet training. Amazingly, a year later, to everyone's surprise, he was ready to join the company in Oslo and, what is more, he actually surpassed his previous standards as far as elevation and turn-out were concerned. Ever since then he has never looked back, after years as a dancer, he still has a distinguished career as a ballet master and répétiteur in Scandinavia, England, Italy and other places in Europe.

\* \* \* \* \*

Although these cases of dancers making a successful and faster recovery were exciting and rewarding this part of my floor practice project wasn't the major point of my interest. From these various positive results it became also obvious that most of these exercises could be helpful to dancers not just after illness or injury but also in their daily striving for a better placement, turn-out, pliability etc. These possibilities captured my curiosity.

The more I taught and coached classical dancers the more I found that many of them—even though they may have outstanding qualities—were forced to struggle throughout their performing life with some kind of physical deficiency. To help with their shortcomings many of these artists—male dancers particularly—were inclined to use sheer force and 'over practice'. This led, more often than not, to injuries.

I knew from my earlier experiences as a student and dancer that special floor exercises executed with the right breathing, may improve some specific problems. So, whenever I coached those with physical shortcomings, I suggested they learn and practise these exercises. At first some dancers were sceptical, particularly about those exercises that had to be executed in parallel and turned-in positions, but quite a few followed my suggestions eagerly and achieved considerable results. (To be fair there were those whom I never succeeded in winning over.)

One of the most enthusiastic and encouraging amongst these dancers was Merle Park, then a young and promising soloist with the Royal Ballet. She needed no persuasion to approach some of her existing physical and technical problems not only within the strict discipline of my classical classes, in which she participated as often as her schedule allowed, but also through my 'unorthodox' ways.

Observing her class work I could easily detect that her special qualities and the brilliance of her technique were somewhat undermined by her beautiful but physically weak feet, and by the fact that one hip joint was far more restricted than the other, which hindered her turn-out. These physical shortcomings were probably due to the polio that she had suffered in her childhood.

When I began coaching her regularly for the ever-increasing (and demanding) roles she was asked to undertake, I gained even more insight into the needs of her finely-tuned physique. After each coaching session I taught her some exercises which, if she did them daily—which she did— I hoped would improve those shortcomings and prevent injuries—which they did!

Merle was indefatigable when it came to refining her technical skills and artistic quality.

She gave up weekends, holidays, early mornings and late evenings in order to work with me whenever and wherever we could arrange it—in my studio, at the Royal Ballet School studios, in her small flat in Holland Park, even on occasion in the crush barre at the Royal Opera House! Her open-minded attitude, insatiable appetite for learning and bettering herself as well as her wonderful achievements and fast progress encouraged me to do further experimental work throughout the following years.

Naturally I was very much aware that we had to be cautious otherwise all this extra work on top of her increasingly demanding schedule within the company could easily lead to her over-tiring herself. I felt it was my duty to prevent any consequent harm.

I've always firmly believed that a dancer's best protection against fatigue-caused injury is to give them well-constructed classes as well as enforcing correct breathing during the daily practice, rehearsals and performances—the only way to have a constant flow of energy during dancing. Nevertheless, I've felt when dancers were over-working or under pressure, some additional prevention was paramount. It occurred to me that introducing to her regular practice some special warm-up and specific corrective exercises—which would not use up a dancer's precious energy while giving them maximum pliability—might do the trick.

Apart from working on sensible warm-up and cool-down exercises I created quite a number of energy-saving 'manipulative' ones where the dancer was doing minimal work while the teacher manipulated his/her limbs, feet and torso and, in some instances, the dancer would be asked to work against the teacher's gently resistant movements.

I introduced these exercises to Merle and she found them so helpful—particularly the manipulative ones—that she often found a way for us to do them just before a general rehearsal or performance as well as during our coaching sessions. It was reassuring that during the many years I coached her she became infinitely stronger, more turned out and, in spite of her demanding schedule, free from injury.

* * * * *

At the time when I was coaching Merle Park many other soloists from the Royal Ballet, London Festival Ballet, National Ballet of Canada, Australian Ballet and Ballet Rambert worked in my studio at my open classes as well as in private coaching sessions. During the latter quite a few of them expressed an interest in learning some of these floor exercises. By teaching them to these dancers, as well as to many of my other students, I had a valuable feedback from a wide cross-section of the profession. These circumstances gave me a further opportunity to collect more information about classical dancers' specific needs in the corrective and rehabilitation areas.

In the following years I was a guest teacher for the Grand Ballet du Marquis de Cuevas and the Royal Winnipeg Ballet. My floor and manipulative exercises proved to be quite useful on many occasions and were welcomed by grateful individuals whatever their rank, age or sex.

Whether in my studio or working with an ensemble I always taught this kind of work in an intimate 'one to one' situation so that I could cater for the individual's specific needs. This was taken for granted—that is—until I started teaching, as a guest, with the Royal Swedish Ballet.

Their prima ballerina, Marianne Orlando, had just returned from maternity leave and, according to her doctor, was fit enough to start her rehabilitation with some gentle barre exercises which she did diligently every day first by herself and then later she tried to join the barre practice within the company classes. After a couple of weeks she still felt uncomfortable, and started to suffer from pain in her lower back and hip joint. She asked for my help.

I noticed that her body, which prior to her pregnancy had been perfectly placed, was not quite in alignment. Her pelvis was in a slightly twisted position that hindered her from working correctly. If she continued her classical training she would have risked serious injury. I suggested that she should seek medical help and, in the mean time, instead of doing her daily classical barre practice, do only some of my floor exercises. We did this for about a week until Brian McDonald, then artistic director of the company, summoned me to his office.

"With all respect, I am afraid that you have created quite a drama by giving Orlando special coaching. She is singing praises about your 'magical' floor exercises but, you see, she is not the only girl here who has just had a baby, right now we have at least a half a dozen of them in this company. Therefore the special 'post-natal' lessons to Marianne are causing a big upheaval. The young mothers are in revolt! I've just had a petition from these 'jealous Amazons', supported by the company's union representative, saying that such individual treatment is not among the privileges usually given to mothers—therefore they demand that all of them should be included in Orlando's post-natal floor-work session. Of course, this must be your own decision entirely but, if you would consider their request favourably, you would have all our thanks, the girls' for getting something they need and want, and mine for helping to keep peace within the company!"

Until now, it never crossed my mind that catering for Orlando's specific needs and helping her individual problem could ever be considered as a kind of 'post-natal' lesson for ballet dancers. Nor did I know that within the company there were several other female dancers who were in the same boat as Marianne. However, I liked the idea that, instead of struggling along with classical classes, exercising on the floor would be a safer and healthier approach in their rehabilitation procedure. Therefore I accepted happily his proposal.

A few days later I was given the use of a large, empty office—the two ballet studios were always otherwise occupied—and I started my special floor class for about five young mothers. It was the first time I had taught this kind of work in a situation that was not 'one to one'. It was again a new challenge but, as there were so few of the participants and their problems were rather similar (although each birth is unique and it must affect each individual body differently), it wasn't too difficult to adapt my ideas to these new circumstances except for the manipulative exercises. These I decided to teach in such a way that they had to learn both the dancer's role as well as the teacher's. Gradually they were able to execute these tasks in pairs, interchanging roles.

Though I had been told of the Royal Swedish Ballet's pregnancy record, I still found it extraordinary that after my 'post-natal' classes had been in operation for a few days the number of mothers expanded rapidly. It was even more surprising when a couple of male dancers presented themselves at the beginning of a lesson and, while the girls could hardly control their laughter, asked if they could take part in the class.

"You may join if you can prove you were recently pregnant," I chuckled.

"Well, that would be a bit difficult! But what about some of these ladies who are impostors themselves?"

"What do you mean?" I asked, pretending to be naïve. There was a hush then giggling and blushing amongst the ladies. Finally one of them admitted, apologetically, "Please forgive us. Indeed, some of us are kind of cheating. We haven't given birth recently but we are injured, unfit for ballet class for quite a while, and when we heard about these lessons they seemed like a God-sent opportunity to us. We thought it wouldn't make any difference to you...."

"O.K. But what about these gentlemen?"

"The same here, we are also injured. Please, don't be angry with us. We thought you wouldn't mind if we joined in, too."

"Not at all. As a matter of fact it is most flattering to see that one's efforts are so much appreciated. I would be quite willing to give it a go but I am a bit worried about simultaneously teaching dancers who, for the moment, might all have different physical needs. Before I can make up my mind I would like to know which of you are the 'genuine' post-natal cases, and I also need to have the exact information on the injuries from which the rest of you are recuperating. If and when I can be assured that your various conditions are compatible, I might be able to work out an exercise programme which will suit most of you, if not all, without running any risks of further damage."

After obtaining the precise description of their ailments I was satisfied that it would be possible to select a number of exercises from which all of them could benefit and practise together without endangering their healing—these were mainly exercises working on their necks, shoulders, diaphragm as well as the abdominal, back and buttock muscles. In addition I prepared exercises which some could easily adapt by practising them in a slightly different position—standing, sitting, kneeling, etc.—in order to avoid aggravating their injury.

At first I conducted the class at a relatively comfortable pace that enabled the dancers to learn both the exercises and how to execute them with a controlled breathing technique. As they were all classically trained this was a most unusual way for them to exercise their bodies. When they learnt the movements together with the correct breathing and understood what each movement was for and how some of them could be adapted to suit a specific problem, I was able gradually to speed up the class and demand more physical output from them.

Soon they were strong and supple enough to join my classical classes with some confidence but it was noticeable that most of those ladies who had recently given birth needed a longer time to regain and control their turn-out and correct balletic stance. Perhaps there was a need for something special and additional to the remedial, conditioning and corrective exercises I was teaching to them—a kind of specific floor practice that could serve and support even more needs of these ballet dancers.

For quite a while I have toyed with the idea of creating special exercises, which would be strongly related to, as well as complementing, the classical ballet technique—a kind of 'floor barre'. However, I felt that such a programme would need time to mature in my mind, tried out on my own physique first and then, only after these preparations had been completed successfully, should it be taught. For the time being I stored my thoughts and observations on this subject, leaving them to mature until, one day...

Working as a ballet mistress to the Vienna State Opera Ballet, I was rushing through the 'Old Town' to the Theater an der Wien for a ballet workshop rehearsal when I tripped and fell over. My heel has lodged in a hole in the cobbled pavement. My ankle was dislocated, the ligament was damaged and the fourth metatarsal was broken. My leg had to be put in a plaster cast. On the next day I was back at the theatre for a demonstration lecture on 'A Classical Dancer's Technique'. You can imagine the effect on the workshop audience that my dramatic entrance had, hobbling on stage with the aid of a couple of crutches!

After five weeks the plaster was removed and I started to move the foot again but it soon became obvious that an operation on the tendon was required, which took place a few weeks later. I spent another month with another smaller, lighter plaster and, once again, this was followed by a long rehabilitation time. Altogether, my recovery took nearly five months.

This unfortunate state of affairs would have made me very miserable, but this period as an invalid turned out to be the 'perfect' occasion to realise my wished-for but procrastinated enterprise.

My new situation allowed me to become my own most suitable guinea-pig for the new floor practice project, because I was able to experience (and survive) the effects of different types of crutches and sticks, the correctly (and incorrectly) fitted plaster casts of differing length, texture and weight, plus the hard and soft hospital beds which caused neck and back aches. I had it all!

I used my misfortune to my advantage and worked consistently on this programme. The various phases of my prolonged convalescence covered a number of variations of those troublesome situations in which injured dancers need the help of a well-constructed floor exercise regime. For me the perfect 'scenery, costumes and props' were at my disposal so that I could understand and feel at first hand what kind of exercises would be useful and feasible for the different periods of rehabilitation.

I carefully planned my daily exercises that were carried out on the bed and later on the floor. I made notes. During my first recovery period my mother came from Hungary to stay for a few weeks. She was a bit shocked when she saw me for hours on end down on the sitting-room floor looking quite grotesque in my heavy plaster cast while practising some *tendus* and *grands battements* while lying on my back, side or tummy. All these weird-looking movements were written down afterwards.

As she helped me to push the furniture out of the way so I would have enough floor space in which to 'wriggle'—as she called the numerous movements I used to loosen the hip joints—she hid her astonishment with an impish smile while saying, "I see, dear, you must be choreographing the 'Dance of the Maggots'." After a while when she became used to the set-up, she just remarked, "Oh, you are up to your 'maggoting' again, are you?!"

For an innocent outsider my efforts must have looked strange, but I was making good progress in establishing a systematically built up regime orientated towards a classical dancer's needs. As it took shape it seemed logical that this system should be called 'floor barre' as the movements practised on the floor were an adaptation, variation and addition to the classical ballet barre exercises.

Back in London after my operation, I let a few friends in the profession know of my project, which had occupied my mind and body for such a long time. They all agreed that there was a great need for this kind of a programme and enthusiastically welcomed it. The keenest and most encouraging amongst them was my dear old friend, author and critic Fernau Hall, who understood and appreciated the purpose and goal of my project more than anybody else. When I explained in more detail the connection I wished to build between the classical barre work and these specific floor exercises, to my great surprise, he exclaimed, "Then you seem to base your work on the same principle as Boris Kniaseff in his '*Barre à terre*', don't you?"

A bomb couldn't have caused more of a shock than his words, but Fernau, carried away in his eagerness, didn't notice this and continued excitedly, "How very interesting! How and why do you differ from his system?"

"I am afraid I can't answer that. If the basic principles of Kniaseff's work and mine are similar it must be sheer coincidence," I muttered in embarrassment. "I'm ashamed to admit but I had no idea that a 'Barre à terre' existed. In my ignorance I thought the whole concept of building a floor practice on the base of a classical barre was an original idea, a 'patent' of mine."

"Oh dear! I am sorry. The Kniaseff System is fairly new and is not yet known internationally but it is quite popular amongst French dancers. I took it for granted that when you were working with the Ballet de Cuevas in France you might have witnessed it being taught, or at least have heard about the principal idea on which it is based."

"Unfortunately not! I must have been too much preoccupied with my work. Besides, at that time I wasn't really interested in the subject. When I did become involved I must have been so immersed in my own ideas that it didn't even occur to me to check if there was any existing work of this kind. I should have done some research, become better informed, so I could decide if there was any point in my working on this project at all. I could be accused of plagiarism. I had better give up the whole thing."

"Nonsense! That would be foolish and hasty. There is always room for these sorts of contributions, especially in connection with a comparatively new system. There is no reason to feel ridiculous. The fact that both of you decided to base floor practice on a classical technique only proves that it must be practical and that there is need for it amongst classically trained dancers. You are not a thief; just accept that Kniaseff was ahead of you. What really matters in the profession is the way you approached and executed the concept."

"Based on the same principle idea, there are bound to be too many similarities."

"You don't know that yet, do you? Surely, there will be similarities as well as differences, all of which help progress and make better results. Instead of giving it all up you should find out as much as you can about his system, and as soon as you can. Then you'll be able to compare and assess both systems for what they are worth."

"Of course, I'll do that some day but not just yet. In spite of my curiosity it would be better for me to remain ignorant of his system for the time being."

"I don't understand you! Just a few minutes ago you were upset because you discovered there was another system about which you knew nothing, similar to the one you have been working on. Now you know it, and could easily study it, you want to ignore it for an indefinite length of time. Why do you want to stay blindfolded?"

"Well, you see, I have already finished building the framework and filled it out with a selection of exercises from already existing material and also my specially created exercises. To this foundation I've added some more sophisticated layers for more advanced levels. I've progressed so far on my own that there are two alternatives I should consider. Either I pack it all up or I carry on without being influenced by other methods and systems. I need to put my work to the test by teaching it to dancers and students at different levels, observe its short and long term results, and make amendments where they are necessary. It might take a long, long time but I'll take off my blinkers only when I am convinced by the proof of the pudding, and not before."

Perhaps my words sounded self-confident enough to pacify Fernau but, deep down, I still had serious doubts.

A year passed during which I continued teaching in the company in Vienna and I didn't even think of my floor barre. I felt I needed to have a rest from it, for the time being, no matter whether I continued to develop it further in the future or decided to abandon it for good.

On my return to London the then director of the Royal Academy of Dancing Teacher Training College, Joan McKenzie, asked me to give a series of ballet classes for the second and third year students. She strongly believed that it would be beneficial for students to occasionally partake in classes that are conducted differently from the usual R.A.D. syllabus.

A Greek girl, Christina Beskou, stood out from all the other students. She had a better technique, possessed a strong personality and an extremely pliable body. It was obvious that her foremost interest was not in teaching but in dancing, and she had the talent for it. After I had finished my guest teaching on the course she obtained permission from the director to take open classes as well as private lessons with me during her free time and in the holidays.

Towards the end of the summer term she arrived one day at my studio, limping heavily and with a bandaged knee the size of a melon. During her morning class she had slipped and landed badly from a big jump, injuring the ligaments in her knee. We both knew this meant a long and complete rest for the leg. Her plans to study with me in the holiday had come to naught. She was devastated. It seemed that the best solution was for her to return to her home on the island of Hydra where rest, gentle exercises in the sea, and the hot climate could all promote her healing.

A few weeks later my husband and I followed her as her parents had invited us to stay in their family home for the rest of the summer. Their tireless hospitality, as well as the outstanding beauty of the unpolluted island, promised a perfect holiday—except my enjoyment was spoilt on those occasions when I found Christina sulking because I had told her off as she had been doing some barre exercises, in spite of the swelling, inflammation and pain.

I wanted her to understand that if she continued exercising through her pain (which she thought—as so many young dancers do—to be the correct professional behaviour) she would hinder the healing process, indeed, probably do further harm, perhaps even some chronic damage to the knee. However, all my lecturing and scolding was useless. I realised that for her own good I must play a trick on this determined, stubborn 'fanatic'.

I proposed a deal. If she promised to stop exercising on her own (I knew that if she gave me her word she would stick to it) I would look after her daily practice, but I didn't tell her at that point that any weight-bearing exercise would be absolutely out of the question.

Christina and her parents were extremely happy with this agreement, until the following day, when the girl realised that instead of her beloved ballet lessons she would do nothing but weird-looking exercises whilst lying or sitting on the sitting-room floor. She was bitterly disappointed and hated every minute of it (and so did my husband and I because I had to leave him, and the cool beach, to fulfil my 'commitment' to Christina, teaching her inside a stifling hot house on scorching summer afternoons.) Nonetheless, a deal was a deal and, whether we liked it or not, we both had to stick to this regime.

So, Christina worked dutifully but without any motivation trying to make me sense that she didn't like the substance of these lessons and also because she hoped that, sooner or later, I might take pity and let her practise in the vertical position. As almost a year had passed since I gave up teaching and working on my floor barre, for 'restarting' this project I could have done with a somewhat more enthusiastic and encouraging atmosphere instead of having to put up with a 'neglected' husband and a sulking student behaving as she was 'serving hard labour!'

I should have felt utterly guilty but I was unmoved by this silent protest and by pretending not to notice it I was just sticking to my guns. After several classes, her intelligence gradually took over and she understood that if she wanted to heal her injury and get back to dancing soon—and this was the most important thing she wanted from life—these exercises were here to enhance her chances. Her working spirit changed and she started practising to the best of her ability.

Our efforts were richly rewarded. For me, it was a joy to watch my system being executed by such a capable physique. Her suppleness actually inspired me to experiment further in inventing new exercises for a more advanced level. For Christina it was also a great satisfaction that she recuperated relatively quickly and she was able to continue her ballet studies much sooner than the most optimistic medical forecast had predicted.

Perhaps these good results let Christina forgive me for the trick I played on her. Little did she know that later in her professional life she was going to become the front rank promoter of the very work—the floor barre—which she hated so much at that time!

During her early dancing career in Greece and Holland, Christina toured a lot with small companies. To her distress she found that on many of the tours the studios were either totally unsuitable (sometimes even non existent!) for either a ballet class or a warm-up before or between performances. It was however, much easier to find a few square feet of floor space backstage or in a corridor or dressing-room (or even in a hotel room) so, in order to prevent injuries, she often had to fall back on the good old floor barre.

Her 'strange practice' as well as her freedom of injury was noted (and envied) by her fellow dancers. They asked her to teach them this system, which she did with my permission, and ever since she has been 'hooked' on it. From that time Christina has taught it consistently with great success in seminars, summer courses and regular schools as a guest teacher all over Europe, and in her own studio in Athens. We are regularly in contact, exchanging thoughts and experiences in connection with this work's development and I have watched her teaching it in London as well as in Athens, with great delight...

* * * * *

When I assessed the results of the various remedial floor exercises and considered what extra benefits could be achieved when they are amalgamated with my own floor barre, I could see that my previous scruples were uncalled for. I felt it was worthwhile to continue teaching this combined system whenever there was a need for it.

To abandon my system, simply because I had discovered belatedly that Boris Kniaseff had based his work on similar principles, made no sense. There was no need to have any fear about the possible similarities and differences of our ideas and their execution as long as these methods worked successfully. Why shouldn't two (or even more) floor barre systems operate alongside one another? To the dancers and students who are in the need of practising these exercises it hardly matters who actually invented them or in what historical order. For those who benefit the only thing that counts is the result. During the following years whenever the necessity arose I continued to teach and elaborate on my system.

When I am asked by injured people to help them when they most need it, my duty, as a teacher, is to do so as there is no risk to their health. Now that I had at hand my floor barre—which had already gained safer and faster results for ballet dancers than rehabilitation exercises on their own—I was in a privileged position to carry out this most important task. Consequently, all worries about the system's 'originality' became irrelevant. The feedback, stimulation and reassurance from the dancers and students whom I taught gave me renewed confidence of its efficiency.

Soon after the episode with Christina I had another valuable though completely different type of feedback from an unexpected source.

Dr. Richard Ralph, then the newly appointed director of the London School of Contemporary Dance, invited me to take over as Head of Ballet from the retiring Molly Lake. This job seemed to be most interesting and full of challenge so I took it with great hope and enthusiasm.

I was intrigued by the possibility of teaching classical ballet technique to talented but mostly untrained adult students in the space of three school years without running the risk of damaging their physique and avoiding 'distortion' or 'vulgarisation' of the traditional classical positions, poses and lines.

At the time of joining this organisation a great number of students—and even some prominent staff members—still had a dislike, disrespect or even ridicule towards ballet. I suspected that in most cases part of their obvious hostility against classical ballet technique was a kind of 'sour grapes' because for most untrained adults the precise execution of it proved to be too difficult a task. I knew that I must change this situation otherwise I would fail in my goals. Since I highly valued contemporary dance culture I felt the challenge to be worthwhile and began my work with great hopes although I was prepared for the teething problems that were bound to occur with such a controversial task.

I attempted to find my way into this labyrinth by suggesting various schemes. These were projects which I thought to be suitable for incorporation into the general aims of the school and which would enhance not only the students' interest in studying a classical ballet technique but also raise the artistic level when teaching this subject to these specially trained students. Amongst these schemes there was one that was connected with the school's tutorial system. Although my suggestion wasn't very popular with the staff, for a short experimental period I was given a chance to go ahead with my ideas.

Originally the school's tutorial sessions were devised to bring the teachers and director into a close relationship with the students and this was achieved with great success. They had discussions on all kinds of subject matters, visited exhibitions, listened to lectures and so on. The idea being that these meetings could be used for all kinds of informative purposes—anything except for the advancement of their dance technique. Although I recognised this to be an excellent system and fully agreed with its principle of getting to know each student personally as well as catering for their intellectual requirements, in the given circumstances I felt that I needed to use these tutorials differently—at least for the time being.

As the majority of students were having enormous difficulties in understanding and executing classical ballet techniques I couldn't resist the temptation of using these intimate tutorials as practical coaching sessions aimed at assisting them to overcome their aversion and shortcomings. During these sessions I encouraged them to show me any of the technical problems they experienced in their ballet studies (in the tutorial sessions I met first and second year students whom otherwise I didn't teach) and then we worked on them. They were most grateful to have a chance for some extra coaching and help in this 'dreaded' subject, which to many seemed to be unattainable.

In contrast to ballet pupils these students had had no possibility at all of developing from childhood onwards such a demanding technique and their only hope of obtaining it without injury within a relatively short time was to use their intelligence.

From their requests it became quite clear that the majority of their problems stemmed from not understanding which muscles to use and how to control them in order to achieve an adequate turn-out and a correct balletic posture—the base for leg extensions, *pirouettes* and elevation together with the right breath control. Not knowing these fundamental issues hindered any co-ordination of *port de bras* with the leg and foot work and trying to sort out all this muddle put them under such mental stress (no wonder they disliked the subject) that it hardly left any room for such things as style, presentation and quality.

In order to understand and execute classical ballet movements correctly they needed to be given a detailed analysis and then to practise them at a much slower space than normal, almost in slow motion. However, daily practice taught in this manner would slow down the ballet lesson to such an extent that the dancers couldn't warm-up their muscles adequately nor gain sufficient stamina—grounds for a hotbed of injuries. This danger was threatening specifically the first and second year students who started their day with the classical class. This is why I thought that the tutorial sessions would be ideal for this type of slow, corrective work and I set out to prove that my ideas were right.

I soon found that some problematic movements done in such slow motion were either strenuous or impossible when done in a vertical stance. So I rearranged them for a sitting position or lying on the floor, which helped these students. In these well-supported and safe postures they found it easy to synchronise the mental understanding with the physical execution, first slowly and then at the correct speed. After these had been worked out in 'weight-supported' positions they found it much easier to put them into practise while standing up.

At first I used this method only for the analysis of the more complex movements but later realised that it had a lot of potential in correcting the basic elements of the ballet technique. Therefore, I taught them the purely classical part of my floor barre as this served my purpose extremely well—it also helped their turn-out and posture. Those few students who belonged to my special tutorial group made good progress and, consequently, began to enjoy their ballet lessons.

After this good start the next step in my scheme should have been to extend these methods beyond the tutorial group. However, for various reasons, I was asked to stop the experiment. Although I firmly believed that teaching classical ballet technique to these adult students was more effective (and safer) with the help of my floor barre, this was not given a further chance. My plan to have the system taught to all the students at the school was shipwrecked before it had even set sail.

At the time I was disappointed and considered the experience to be a complete waste of time, a fiasco, but in hindsight I value it differently. The experiment may have been short-lived and incomplete but while it lasted it certainly helped the progress of a few young contemporary dancers. In fact, not only those who took part in my tutorials benefited, a number of other students who had heard about the good effects of my floor barre decided to learn it and then kept practising it. I, too, learned a lot. Indirectly, these experiments gave me much information about the special needs and problems of adult students and contemporary dancers. By monitoring their reactions I had some favourable response considering my floor barre.

* * * * *

From the many ballet dancers who learnt my floor barre during the following years the most valuable feedback I have had has been from one of my long-time pupils, Josephine Jewkes. As her private teacher and coach since the early eighties I have followed her career closely—from student, through the process of developing into a ballerina and her later diversion into the contemporary scene. During these eventful years, like so many others of her calibre and status, she couldn't escape the occasional injuries of various types and seriousness.

When touring in Ronald Hynd's new production of *The Sleeping Beauty* she sustained a serious knee injury. The medical experts all seemed to have different diagnoses so she received in succession a variety of treatments. The pain was insistent and prevented her from dancing for a long time. When she returned to London and asked for my assistance I introduced my floor barre to her, hoping that it would nurse her back to strength with comparative safety and speed. Right from the first lesson she took it surprisingly well. As we proceeded she gradually became a keen believer in its benefits and even recorded our sessions on video—a reminder in case she might need to use it when on tour.

From this time, whenever she was hurt, she consistently made use of this floor practice in addition to all the medical help given by English National Ballet (and later, Rambert Dance Company), insisting that it accelerated and ensured a safer recovery. She was so convinced of its good effects that she has often recruited other dancers, and even physiotherapists, to learn and make use of the system.

Josephine also called my attention that when she practised my floor barre for a long period—apart from rehabilitation purposes—she had noticed that the exercises actually improved her turn-out, posture and stamina. I had not mentioned to her so far that these were results I had hoped for. It was most encouraging that my secret intentions proved to be right.

It didn't take long for her to understand that if she applied and adapted to her work in daily classical classes and rehearsals the basic principles of breath control within the system it would benefit her technique and stamina during performances... (and—let's face it—that issue is not an unimportant one in a dancer's life!).

She arranged for Tim Almaas (her partner on and off stage) to join her in some of these lessons, although he had no need of any rehabilitation. From their questions and the positive comments they made in the after-class discussions it seemed that they considered the potential of my floor barre to be more than just a mere exercise programme for injured dancers. They became convinced that this system should be introduced in vocational schools during a young dancer's training process.

Tim reckoned, "Students should have the opportunity to learn and practise regularly these exercises in order to correct some physical imperfections and weaknesses. These could prevent some of those acute and chronic injuries they pick up at school and in a future professional life."

Josephine added, "I wish your floor barre had been created when I was a young student. Lots of my later problems could probably have been avoided!"

Indeed, ever since I started working on my floor barre it occurred to me that if it was practised regularly during dance training from an early age—and not just at the time of rehabilitation—it might well become just as useful for young vocational students as well as the numerous amateur pupils. It could be part of a healthy preparation and a safe exercise programme before and during classical ballet studies if certain modifications were carried out according to the age and ability of the youngsters.

\* \* \* \* \*

Meanwhile, Christina Beskou—who has been teaching my system to many different types of student over many years—has kept me informed regularly about her successes and interesting observations. While I have had the opportunity of conveying my floor barre to, mainly, professional dancers at the time of injury on a 'one to one' basis and evaluated its effect through the results, she has concentrated on teaching it in special 'floor barre open classes' mostly for healthy adult students and has drawn her conclusions from them.

Her pupils have differing backgrounds and aims. The majority are young professionals, students of various vocational schools (some trained in ballet, others more familiar with contemporary dance) and talented 'late starters'. In spite of their divers preparation and qualifications they keep flocking to these classes because they find they gain much from them as far as muscle-control, body posture, turn-out, extension, suppleness and stamina are concerned.

Christina teaches my floor barre to a number of amateurs as well. It seems they are interested in it because they find it enjoyable and a thorough way of exercising their bodies with a very low risk of injury compared to the various 'work out' and 'keep fit' systems on offer.

My floor barre, however, evolved over many years of working with professional dancers trained in classical ballet techniques. Consequently, it was natural to consider a classical ballet dancer's needs first. I adapted it for the requirements of contemporary dancers and students at a later date. Although it did cross my mind that this system might become useful for teaching amateurs as well, I didn't work out a programme suitable for their needs, as I was not teaching this type of student. Finding out from Christina that this system was also proving to be easily adaptable, effective and popular with her adult amateurs was therefore quite pleasing and thought provoking.

It occurred to me that as the floor barre, by its true nature, seemed to help even adult and untrained students to comprehend the sophisticated and 'un-natural' physical demands of a classical ballet technique—it also helps them strengthen physical weakness and inefficiency as well as correcting bad habits and postures in a safe and protecting way—it could be just as useful in preparing the delicate physique of young children for the stressful, physical and mental demands of both classical ballet and contemporary dance disciplines.

In other words, instead of considering the floor barre only as a suitable system for the purpose of rehabilitation, or a corrective and conditioning one, it might be looked on as a method of preventing students from sustaining injuries. If, in teaching it to the many children who start dancing early in their lives, we can help them to understand and perform their tasks better, faster and safer, then it could develop into a form of protection from injuries caused by physical shortcomings, incorrect breathing or, simply, intellectual immaturity.

This latter problem—I have discussed it in great detail in my book *Mind Over Body*—often affects the very young but, most of the time, it is overlooked. Children develop incorrect postures and other harmful habits—a typical cause for injury—because they are encouraged to exercise only their bodies; their brains are left out of the learning procedure. If, during classes, only the children's instinct for imitation is evoked but their intelligence is left unmotivated one cannot expect them to understand and register corrections while performing the required movements. It is important to realise that mastering images of the floor barre (including correct breathing) helps them mentally to understand and physically execute better the requirements of a dancer's correct technique.

To rate the results achieved with the floor barre only from a physical point of view doesn't conform to my general idea about teaching dance technique of any kind at all. Although I can't claim that my exercise system has any artistic value—indeed, by its nature, none of these corrective and conditioning regimes can have—I aimed at least to create one which enhances the participants' mental capacity to a great extent. So it was satisfying to realise that, without involving the participating students' total mental activity, the physical execution of these exercises is actually quite impossible. Students must be totally alert in order to control the correctness of their technical performance in this exercise programme.

Apart from enhancing mental awareness as far as a dancer's physical output is concerned the floor barre appeared to be a beneficial influence on their emotional life also. This is particularly evident during the trying time of rehabilitation when practising this programme gives those who are often inpatient and frustrated the satisfaction of doing something useful which will help their dance technique. When injured dancers are obliged to stay away from the real action, knowing that their precious time is not wasted but being put to good use is a comforting feeling for them and prevents depression.

Apart from thwarting depression I have also found that another great psychological problem, which often occurs during rehabilitation, can be avoided through use of the floor barre. I have frequently noticed that injured dancers are more than eager to recover in the shortest possible time but, when they finally get the green light from their medical advisor to start regular daily dancing practice, many of them are unconsciously afraid that they may cause further hurt to the injured part of their bodies. Exercising a weakened physique while in such an anxious state of mind tenses up the muscles and makes the body so rigid that relapses, or even new injuries, could occur. However, when they start their recuperation with the floor practice (which will give them more physical support than an ordinary class routine and its inseparable, correct breathing technique will exercise the whole body in a relaxed manner) their recovery period will turn into an optimistic and self-assuring rehabilitation instead of a traumatic experience full of anxiety and nervous tension.

As well as these positive psychological effects for dancers the floor barre practice also is advantageous in ordinary circumstances. In fact, it seems that it can play quite an important role in the lives of physically healthy participants by building up their self-confidence.

Contrary to other conditioning and workout programmes the floor barre is designed particularly to serve the needs of a dancer. It is purpose built: it helps to correct postural faults from a dancer's point of view (postures that may not be necessarily right for everybody, for example for a gymnast, a fashion model, and so on), shaping and strengthening the physique, enhancing the flexibility of the body as well as aiding and supporting dancers' technique and stamina. Therefore, it is satisfying and reassuring for performers and students, and it raises their self esteem and confidence when they realise that their extra effort in learning and practising pays dividends—higher standards and a greater endurance in their classical or contemporary dance technique.

Self esteem and self confidence are the most important elements in forming a young person's positive outlook on life, but when it comes to studying an art form—whether at a vocational or an amateur level—these are the paramount bases on which to build achievements. Apart from the physical advantages the floor barre serves these essential purposes as well.

* * * * *

From the time I was a dancer I always had a strong suspicion that many acute and chronic injuries among students (and specially in the case of professional dancers) may stem from those periods after annual vacations (or Christmas and Easter holidays) when they start daily exercises and rehearsals again.

It is well known in the profession that after several weeks of complete rest a dancer's physique must be 're-tuned', gently and gradually, for the demanding tasks ahead. Teachers in most schools and companies would like this 'golden rule' to be carried out seriously but for various reasons it is often beyond their power. As a teacher I have faced this dilemma several times when engaged with companies connected to an opera house. Once, when I was in Vienna at the beginning of the season and the first performance was in just two weeks time, I geared the company classes accordingly until, after two days only had passed, we learned from the direction the following: "There is a problem. The performance of *Rigoletto* (scheduled in three days time) has to be cancelled so the ballet must fill the gap."

I was alarmed at this decision but my complaints, explanations and pleading to the management were all in vain. Because of the opera house subscription system there had to be a performance and this was the only solution.

Unfortunately, it isn't only artistic ignorance or an opera-minded administration's lack of interest that forces dancers to perform when utterly unprepared and with great risk to their health. I often wonder why some ballet companies will start a season with a repertoire which is physically more demanding for both principal dancers and entire company—*The Sleeping Beauty, Etudes,* etc.—when there are far less taxing and shorter ballets available for their choice, such as those using fewer dancers and a less demanding technique. No wonder that there is a shockingly high percentage of seriously injured dancers by the second or third month of the season!

It similarly happens that in some vocational schools classes for senior students given immediately after a holiday period are often technically too demanding. Teachers and pupils naturally take it for granted that after vacation a certain amount of muscle stiffness is unavoidable. However, the problem is that after the first days only a few of the students are able to differentiate between pain caused by muscle stiffness and a possible minor injury—until too late.

I warn my pupils of these hazards and, in order to prevent trouble, I suggest they start practising my floor barre a few days before the official season begins and continue with a shortened version during the first week before each ballet class. Judging by the results, it seems a richly rewarding investment for them to put in extra effort every new season. At the same time one may come to a conclusion that the floor barre should be used as a potent preventative.

* * * * *

Over the years quite a number of dancers and teachers who have learnt my floor barre have begun to teach it with great enthusiasm. The ball 'started to roll' without any control, a natural procedure in our profession which is full of exercises and systems helpful to dancers. Like a snowball it gathered different particles on its journey and, whether I like it or not, it has often changed its nature. These additions, deductions and alterations may be for the better, and some for the worse. There is always a danger that misinterpreted speed, breathing technique or exercises taught in the wrong order, may cause bad posture, technical faults and injury.

In order to minimalise these misunderstandings and misinterpretations I present on the following pages the written record of my floor barre. I hope that teachers, dancers and students will find it as beneficial and helpful in their work as my followers and I have done in ours.

# PART II

# THE BASIC POSITIONS

# General and Practical Information

The floor barre, like most systems of physical exercise, should be conveyed to students and dancers step by step and with an analytical approach suited to their age, skills and body-structure, always remembering that to begin with, even a principal dancer is a beginner as far as these exercises are concerned.

Most exercises have both simple and more demanding versions to accommodate different standards, needs and ages, by changing the speed, rhythm, emphasis, duration and the way they are combined. There are endless variations.

At the beginning everything should be taught in a simple form and at a rather slow pace. At the same time there are some movements that should be never introduced before the dancer has reached an advanced level. These specific exercises will be pointed out in the forthcoming text when describing them.

Efficient breath control is the basis of a healthy and effective exercise regime and the floor barre should be conveyed and executed with this in mind right from the beginning. With the description of each exercise the suggested breathing is also indicated in detail. However, this can be handled more as a guideline rather than an 'unchangeable rule' depending on the tempo of the exercise and its emphasis.

The purpose of a consciously-used breathing technique is to make dancers understand and experience that if they sensibly manipulate their breathing in and out or hold their breath during all physical tasks, they will save precious energy and, by utilising the oxygen intake and expulsion of carbon-dioxide in the most efficient way, they will achieve better results.

Consequently, according to the situation and needs—which muscle requires strengthening, stretching and loosening, how many times and at what speed an exercise is executed, and the individual's age, skills, strength and stamina—by manipulating the respiration one is also able to change the *purpose* of any given exercise. As each situation is different, the correct breathing has to be considered accordingly. Careful observation and individual experimentation are needed but there is one general rule: breathe in on the upbeat and breathe out for a stretch, also at the summit of sustained movement.

Do not mistake this floor barre for a general warm-up (although a number of exercises put in a certain order and speed can be used as such.) Even in its simplest form it can become more demanding physically than a sensible, general warm-up. Therefore, I suggest starting each floor barre class with a warm-up designed to suit the character of the subsequent floor practice. These exercises will be described in detail under 'Warm-up Exercises'.

These descriptions, as well as the other exercises of the Floor Barre section, are not in the order of how a class should be built up. They are grouped according to the nature of the exercise. For example, all versions and modulations of a *tendu* exercise are indicated as: turned in, turned out, with flexed or pointed feet; likewise positions such as sitting or lying on the back, stomach or side are described one after the other within the group. Of course, during a single class one never executes *all* these permutations, nor in this order. Naturally, other types of exercise—*pliés, ronds de jambes, développés, grands battements*, etc.—are treated likewise.

The building up of a lesson however, is one of the most important factors in achieving lasting and safe results. In Part VI of this book, readers will find notes of a few sample classes at beginner, intermediate and advanced level. These will represent the correct teaching order within a floor barre lesson.

To follow easily the descriptions of the various exercises and to understand how this floor barre is constructed you should note a number of points.

For practical reasons, I suggest that individual soft mats should be used during practice as you may find that some of the exercises might cause considerable discomfort without them, particularly while practising in the 'lying on the stomach' position. At the beginning of these studies to avoid straining the neck and arching the back when lying on your back, it is advisable to rest your head on a small pillow.

# THE BASIC POSITIONS
## Basic Leg and Feet Positions

All these basic leg and feet positions can be used with flexed and pointed feet (**Figure 1/a and 1/b**) in the different body positions (like sitting on the floor, lying on the side or stomach, kneeling, reclining and so on). In addition there are numerous variations of these basic positions according to the specific exercise in question (for example, the ones which are executed in a turned-in version, or in an enlarged 2$^{nd}$ position when sitting, etc.).

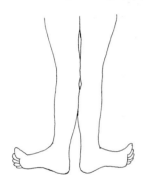

*Figure 1/a*

**a)** 1$^{st}$ position with flexed feet as in classical ballet when standing on the floor

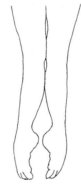

*Figure 1/b*

**b)** 1$^{st}$ position with pointed feet

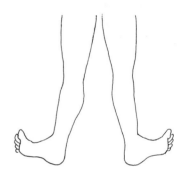

*Figure 1/c*

**c)** 2$^{nd}$ position with flexed feet

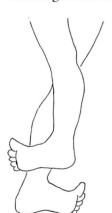

*Figure 1/d*

**e)** 4$^{th}$ position with flexed feet

*Figure 1/e*

**g)** 5$^{th}$ position with flexed feet

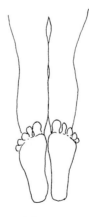

*Figure 1/f*

**i)** 6$^{th}$ position with flexed feet

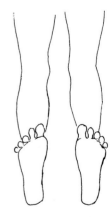

*Figure 1/g*

**k)** Parallel position with flexed feet

# Basic Body Positions

**a) Sitting** on the floor placing the relaxed arms next to the torso with palms on the floor. The legs are stretched forward (in all the positions described and illustrated above in ' Basic Leg and Feet Positions') with upright torso, chest lifted, the neck and head are a straight continuation of the spine, shoulders and chin relaxed (***Figure 2***).

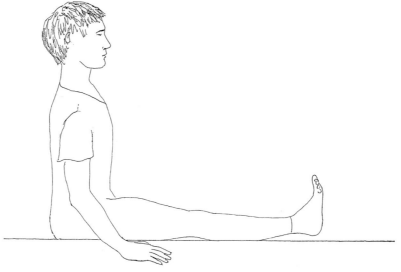

***Figure 2***

**b) Reclining** on the floor with the legs stretched forward (in all the above mentioned leg and feet positions) resting the torso on the lower arms which are placed on the floor behind the torso; the spine controlled in a straight line, chin is relaxed (***Figure 3***).

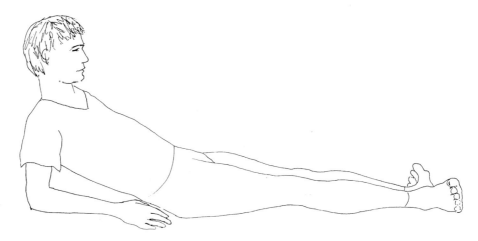

***Figure 3***

**c) Lying on the back** with a small pillow under the head (***Figure 4***).

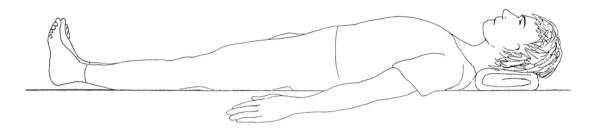

*Figure 4*

**d)** Positions **a, b** & **c** with bent knees while feet are resting flat on the floor (***Figure 5***).

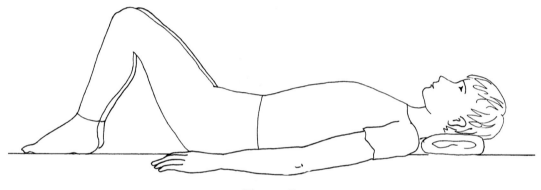

*Figure 5*

**e)  Lying on the side** (left) with a straight spine, head resting on the relaxed left arm, right arm bent with the palm against the floor in front of the chest, with  both legs stretched in a turned-out 1$^{st}$ position with pointed or flexed feet (***Figure 6***).

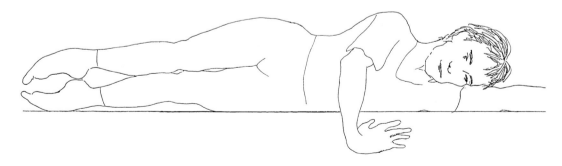

*Figure 6*

**f)** Lying on the left side with the left thigh in a straight line with the hip, lower leg slightly bent for stability, the left foot is pointed while the right leg is straight and turned out either with pointed or flexed foot (**Figure 7**).

*Figure 7*

**g)** **Lying on the stomach** with all the feet and leg positions described and illustrated above. **Note:** All these body positions can be used while resting both feet flat against the wall when one wishes to use the support or resistance of the wall (**Figure 8**).

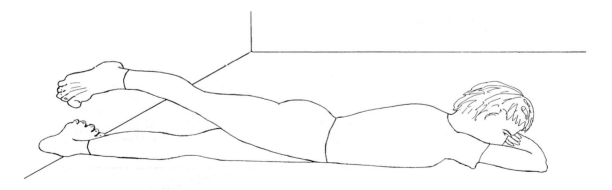

*Figure 8*

In all positions the correct posture needs to be controlled by avoiding:
• arching of the back (*Figure 9*),
• dropping the shoulders forward especially in the reclining and side positions (*Figures 10 & 11*),
• rounding the back and pulling up the shoulders (*Figure 12*).

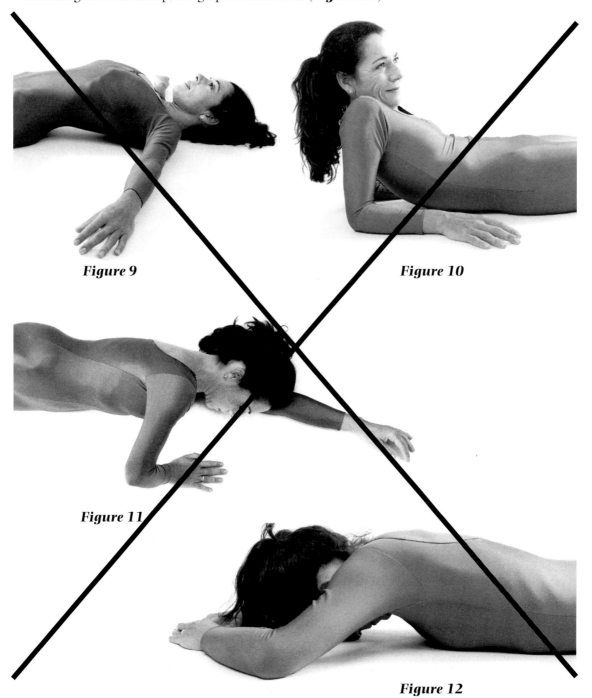

*Figure 9*

*Figure 10*

*Figure 11*

*Figure 12*

# Basic Arm Positions

Besides the five classical ballet arm positions there are additional ones in the Floor Barre as when

## Lying on the back

**a)** In a low diagonal with palms and forearms turned towards the floor (***Figure 13***).

**b)** In a classical 2<sup>nd</sup> position but the forearms and the palms are turned towards the floor (***Figure 14***).

**Figure 13**                                              **Figure 14**

**Note:** Arm positions **a** and **b** should be used especially at the beginning stages as they help to keep the correct torso position and the balance in many of the exercises executed while lying on the back like: *grands battements, grands ronds de jambes, développés* and so on and so forth...

**c)** Both hands below the nape of the neck placing the hands on top of each other between the shoulder blades (***Figure 15***).

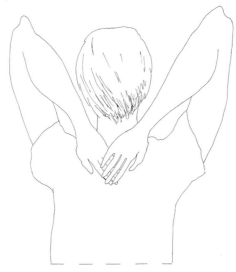

*Figure 15*

## Lying on the side

**d)** Head resting on one arm while other is bent in front of the chest supported by the palm (as illustrated previously when describing 'Body Positions' in ***Figures 6*** **and** ***7***).

**e)** Head resting on the palm of the bent arm (***Figure 16***).

*Figure 16*

**Note:** Position **e** should be used only at the advanced and professional level.

# Lying on the stomach

**f)** Arms resting on the floor with bent elbows so that fingers meet above the head forming a pentagon shape (***Figure 17***).

**g)** Both arms bent and hands placed on top of each other while the chin rests on them (***Figure 18***).

*Figure 17*

*Figure 18*

**h)** Both arms bent and hands placed on top of each other under the forehead (***Figure 19***).

***Figure 19***

**i)** Both arms bent in such a way that the upper arms are resting at shoulder level, while the forearms are at 90° and palms are turned towards the floor (***Figure 20***).

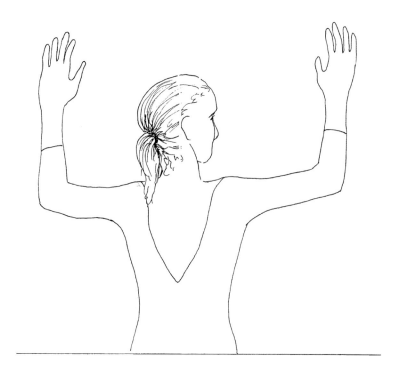

***Figure 20***

# PART III

# THE WARM-UP EXERCISES

# THE WARM-UP EXERCISES

Although some of these warm-up exercises are very simple and physically not demanding—they are suitable to introduce students and dancers to the Floor Barre regime or, in case of rehabilitation, after an operation, long illness, etc.—it is important to practise each basic movement (without any modulations) quite a number of times. At a later stage, according to the dancer's technical standards and intelligence, some of these exercises should be combined with one another (for example: the exercise which mobilises the toes can be amalgamated with that which moves the ankle, and later with the one manipulating the knee, hip-joint, etc.). Ideally, one should aim for a situation where most of the exercises are combined and performed in a long chain of movements with just a few short breaks in between. The fewer times we stop the flow of movements the quicker and more safely the dancer's body will be prepared for more demanding tasks.

It is also important that some of the warm-up exercises—those that relax and mobilise the centre spine gently—should be inserted between the more strenuous exercises of the Floor Barre.

## Mobilising the Toes

**1)** In a sitting position or lying on the back, legs straight in the 6$^{th}$ position and feet relaxed. Turn the toes upwards and breathe in (***Figure 21***); relax toes while holding breath; curl the toes downwards and breathe out ('Parrot's Claws' ***Figure 22***); relax toes while holding breath.

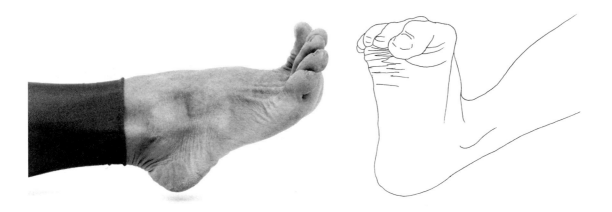

*Figure 21*                    *Figure 22*

**2)** In a sitting position or lying on the back, legs straight in the parallel or 6$^{th}$ position with the feet relaxed. Separate the toes from each other and breathe in (***Figure 23***); relax toes and breathe out.

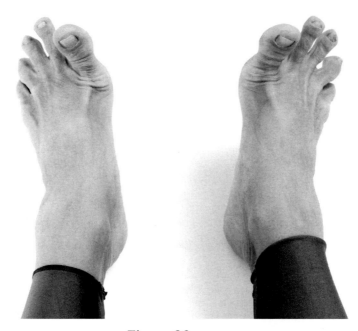

*Figure 23*

## Mobilising the Ankle

**3)** In a sitting position or lying on the back, legs straight in the 6th position. On the up-beat point feet and breathe in. Flex feet and breathe out; hold this position and hold breath; point feet (**Figure 24**) and breathe in; hold this position and hold breath.

***Figure 24***

**4)** In a sitting position or lying on the back, legs in a small 2nd position with relaxed feet. Circle the feet by moving the ankles *en dehors* and breathe in; circle the feet by moving the ankles *en dedans* and breathe out (**Figure 25**).

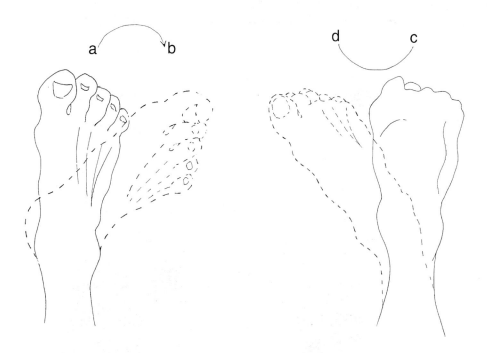

***Figure 25***

## Mobilising the Toes and Ankle simultaneously

**5)** In a sitting position or lying on the back with the legs in a parallel or 6<sup>th</sup> position with the feet relaxed. On the up-beat point feet while separating the toes from one another and breathe in; flex feet while curling the toes tightly under ('parrot's claws') and breathe out. At a somewhat more advanced stage this exercise might be executed in such a way that when the dancer performs the 'parrot's claws' she/he rotates the feet towards each other and, when arching the foot with the upward curled toes, the dancer rotates the feet away from each other.

**6)** Combine exercise **3** with exercise **5**.

**7)** Combine exercise **4** with exercise **5**.

## Mobilising the Arch of the Foot and Toes simultaneously

**8)** In a sitting position or lying on the back with legs in a parallel or 6<sup>th</sup> position. On the up-beat bend knees while the soles of the feet rest on the floor and breathe in. Push stretched toes against the floor while lifting the arches of the feet and pulling them slightly towards the heel and breathe out (***Figure 26***); relax feet whilst holding breath; lift toes upward while raising the arch and flex feet while breathing in; place the soles of the feet on the floor, relax and hold breath.

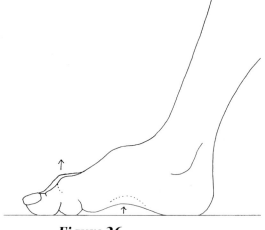

*Figure 26*

**Note:** In the Warm-up as well as in the Floor Barre exercises, whenever the positions of the feet change from pointing to flexing (or vice versa), there are two ways of doing this. At beginners level do it as in classical ballet technique but for a somewhat more advanced level one should practise it as follows: when the ankle starts to move the ball of the foot pushes simultaneously downwards while the toes flex upwards (as already illustrated in exercise **1** (***Figure 21***); then the toes point gradually while the arch of the foot is kept stretched ('curling the feet'). When reversing this procedure the motion starts by moving the ankle upwards with the toes curling upwards while the arch of the foot is stretched all the time.

## Mobilising the Knees and Hip-joints simultaneously

**9)** In a sitting position or lying on the back with legs in 6<sup>th</sup> position. On the up-beat breathe in. Bend both knees while the soles of the feet are kept flat on the floor and breathe out (***Figure 27***). While stretching both knees place legs back on the floor into the starting position.

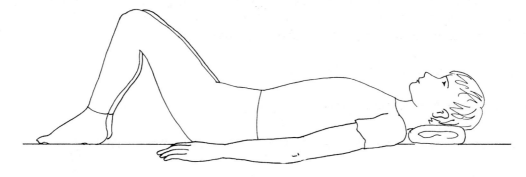

*Figure 27*

**10)** Exercise **9** with pointed feet when bending the knees then flex the feet when stretching them.

**11)** Exercise **10** from a turned out 1<sup>st</sup> position and keep the turn-out during the whole action.

**12)** Lying on the back, legs in the 6<sup>th</sup> position. On the up-beat bend knees and draw the pointed feet closely towards the buttock and breathe in; stretch right leg in the air to a 90° angle and breathe out; drop the lower leg and place the pointed toe on the floor and breathe in. Do the same procedure with the left leg.

**13)** Lying on the back with legs in 6<sup>th</sup> position. On the up-beat lift the right leg with bent knee in the air and hold the thigh with both hands, upper leg at a 90° angle and breathe in; circle the lower leg by moving the right knee *en dehors* and breathe out (***Figure 28***); relax and breathe in. Repeat the exercise *en dedans*. Same with the left leg.

*Figure 28*

## Mobilising the Hip-joint

**14)** Sitting or lying on the back with legs in parallel position with feet pointed. On the up-beat breathe in; turn in right leg and breathe out; turn it back to parallel position and breathe in; turn right leg out and breathe out; turn it back to parallel position and breathe in. The same procedure with the left leg.

**15)** Exercise **14** with pointed foot when turning in and flex them when turning out.

**16)** Exercise **15** executed with slightly bent knee.

**17)** Rotating hip-joint *en dehors*. Lying on the back, legs in parallel position. On the up-beat breathe in; turn in both legs with pointed feet while bending knees slightly and breathe out; keep bending knees while moving them gradually into a parallel position with flexed feet and hold breath; turn out bent knees (as in a 2ⁿᵈ position *demi plié*) and start breathing out; continue breathing out while stretching the turned out knees and point feet. Do the same *en dedans*.

**18)** Lying on the back, legs in 6ᵗʰ position. On the up-beat point both feet. Bend the right knee and leaving the right big toe on the floor draw the leg towards the torso as far as the left knee and breathe in (***Figure 29***);

*Figure 29*

*Figure 30*
turn the right leg in but keep the pelvis perfectly square (in this position the leg can move only at a very limited angle) and breathe out (***Figure 30***);

lift the knee to an upright position and breathe in; turn the leg out (as in a *retiré passé*) and breathe out (**Figure 31**);

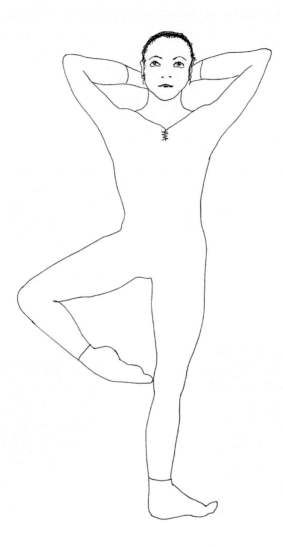

**Figure 31**
lift the knee to an upright position and breathe in. The same procedure with the left leg.

**19)** Sitting or lying on the back with the legs in parallel position. On the up-beat bend knees, resting feet flat on the floor and breathe in; turn in the knees towards each other and breathe out (*Figure 32*); hold this position and hold breath; recover starting position and breathe in.

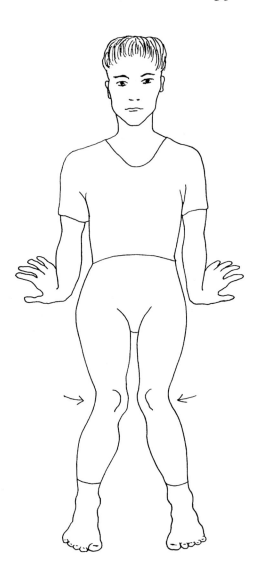

*Figure 32*

## Mobilising the neck

In the next exercises (**20** to **23**) the starting position is the same: sitting on the floor in a wide $2^{nd}$ position (***Figure 33***) while holding the head and spine upright. The wide $2^{nd}$ position **must never be forced** wider than the dancer can achieve without strain and pain.

***Figure 33***

**20)** On the up-beat breathe in: bend the neck forward and breathe out; lift the head upright and breathe in; bend the neck backwards and breathe out; recover the starting position and turn the neck $\frac{1}{8}^{th}$ towards the right with the head facing diagonally and breathe in; bend the neck forward while keeping the head in the diagonal and breathe out; lift the head upright still facing diagonal and breathe in; bend the neck backwards while keeping the head in the diagonal and breathe out; recover starting position in *en face*. Do the same with the head facing left diagonal.

**21)** On the up-beat breathe in; turn the head to the right and breathe out; hold this position and hold breath; turn the head *en face* and breathe in; turn the head to the left and breathe out; hold the position and hold breath; turn the head *en face* and breathe in.

**22)** On the up-beat breathe in; keeping the head *en face* drop it over the right shoulder and breathe out (**Figure 34**); hold this position and hold breath; lift the head upright and breathe in. Same procedure for the other side.

**Figure 34**

**23)** On the up-beat breathe in; starting from the right rotate the neck and roll the head around in a circle while breathing out; lift the head upright into starting position and breathe in. Same for the other side.

## Mobilising the Shoulders

In the following exercises (**24** to **28**) the starting positions can be the same: sitting with a straight spine in either in the 1$^{st}$, 6$^{th}$ or wide 2$^{nd}$ position with the arms placed either next to the torso or bending the elbows and placing the fingertips lightly on the shoulders.

**24)** On the up-beat breathe in; pull shoulders down and breathe out; hold this position and hold breath; bring them back to starting position and breathe in; hold this position and hold breath; lift shoulders up and breathe out; hold this position and hold breath; bring them back to starting position and breathe in.

**25)** On the up-beat breathe in; curl shoulders forward and breathe out; hold this position and hold breath; bring them back to starting position and breathe in; pull shoulders backwards ('pinching' shoulder-blades) and breathe out; hold this position and hold breath; bring shoulders back to starting position and breathe in.

**26)** On the up-beat breathe in; circle shoulders *en dehors* (forwards and breathe out; upwards and backwards and breathe in; downward while gradually breathing out) while keeping the arms relaxed next to the torso. Do the same reversed *en dedans*.

**27)** On the up-beat lift both arms into a 5$^{th}$ position (or place the fingertips onto the shoulders) and breathe in. Execute exercise **26** in such a way that the arms are following the *en dehors* and the *en dedans* circles (as if they were an extension of the shoulders).

**28)** On the up-beat hold hands with relaxed arms behind the torso and breathe in. While keeping the spine straight and the head upright lift the arms as high as possible without forcing and start breathing out; hold this position and continue breathing out; place the arms to starting position and breathe in.

**29)** Sitting in the wide 2$^{nd}$ position. On the up-beat place both arms bent behind the back in such a way that the right hand is touching the left elbow while the left hand is touching the right one and breathe in. Keeping the spine and head erect and motionless lift the arms and simultaneously pull them towards the right and breathe out; hold this position while breathing in; pull the arms towards the left and breathe out; hold this position while breathing in.

## Mobilising the Elbows

In the next exercises (**30** to **36**) the starting position is the same: sitting on the floor (in either 2$^{nd}$ or 6$^{th}$ position) or lying on the back with both arms next to torso.

**30)** On the up-beat breathe in; bend elbows and touch the shoulders lightly with the fingers and breathe out (**Figure 35**); drop arms to starting position and breathe in.

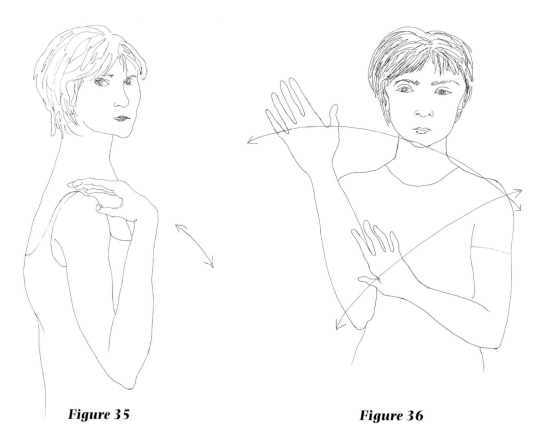

| *Figure 35* | *Figure 36* |

**31)** On the up-beat lift the forearms and breathe in; turn them inwards (palms facing each other) and breathe out; turn them back into the starting position and breathe in; turn forearms outwards and breathe out; turn them back into starting position and breathe in.

**32)** On the up-beat lift the forearms and breathe in; move the forearms like windscreen wipers (**Figure 36**); drop both of them to the right and breathe out; lift them to starting position and breathe in; drop both of them to the left and breathe out; lift forearms to the starting position and breathe in.

**33)** On the up-beat lift forearms and breathe in; circle them by moving elbows *en dehors* and breathe out. Do the same *en dedans*.

## Mobilising the Wrists

**34)** On the up-beat lift the forearms and breathe in; flex hands with palm upwards and breathe out; hold this position and hold breath; lift hands and breathe in; drop the hands with palm turned downwards and breathe out; hold this position and hold breath; lift hands and breathe in.

**35)** On the up-beat lift right forearm with palm facing forward while left hand is holding firmly under the right wrist and breathe in; drop right hand to the right (***Figure 37***) and breathe out; lift right hand to the starting position and breathe in; drop right hand to the left and breathe out; lift right hand to the starting position and breathe in. Same for the left hand.

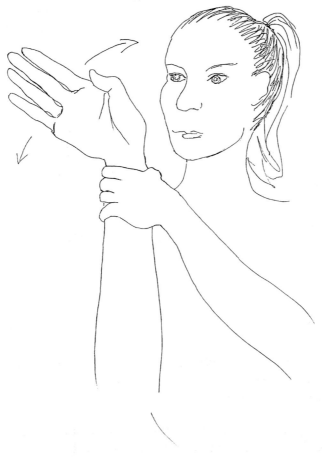

***Figure 37***

**36)** Upper arms are resting next to the torso. On the up-beat lift the forearms and breathe in; circle the hands by moving the wrist *en dehors* and gradually breathe out; rest in the starting position and breathe in. Same procedure *en dedans*.

## Mobilising the spine

**37)** Sitting on the floor with legs and arms in a wide 2nd position. On the up-beat turn palms downwards and breathe in; turn the torso (including the head) to the right and at the same time bend and turn in the left knee gently and breathe out; hold this position and hold breath; recover to starting position and breathe in. The same to the left.

**38)** Exercise **37** but with the head always facing forward (**Figure 38**);

*Figure 38*

**39)** Sitting on the floor with legs in a wide 2nd position. On the up-beat lift arms to the 5th position and breathe in; bend sideways to the right as low as possible and hold breath (**Figure 39**); hold this position and breathe out; straighten up to starting position while gradually breathing in. The same procedure to the left.

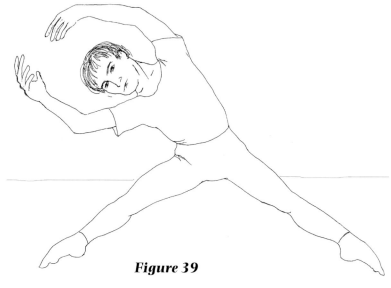

*Figure 39*

**40)** Kneeling on all fours in the 6ᵗʰ position (**Figure 40**);

**Figure 40**

On the up-beat breathe in; drop the head downwards and simultaneously push the centre-spine upwards producing a curve while gradually breathing out (**Figure 41**);

**Figure 41**

lift the head while arching the back and breathe in gradually (***Figure 42***).

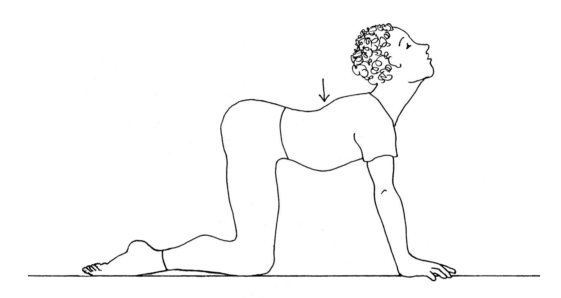

***Figure 42***

**41)** Exercise **40** executed in such a way that while curving the centre-spine upwards the knees are bent more and the bottom lowered towards the heels; (***Figure 43***);

***Figure 43***

while arching the back bend the elbows and pushing the torso forward lower the chest towards the floor (*Figure 44*).

*Figure 44*

**42)** Kneeling on all fours in the 6ᵗʰ position. On the up-beat breathe in; swing the pelvis to the right and breathe out (*Figure 45*);

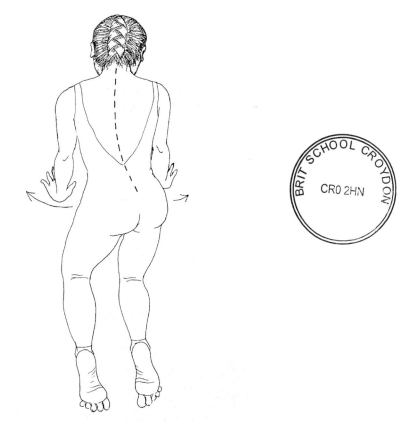

*Figure 45*

bring it back to the starting position and breathe in; swing the pelvis to the left and breathe out; come back to the starting position and breathe in.

**43)** Lying on the back or on the stomach with the legs in 6ᵗʰ position with pointed feet, arms in the 5ᵗʰ position. On the up-beat breathe in; elongate from the sockets the right leg and arm for a few centimetres and breathe out (***Figure 46***); hold this position and hold breath; recover to starting position and breathe in. The same procedure with the left leg and arm.

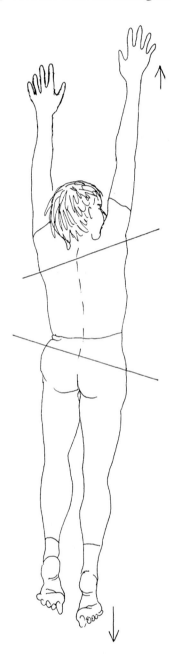

***Figure 46***

**44)** Lying on the stomach in the 6<sup>th</sup> or 1<sup>st</sup> position while the arms are either resting alongside the torso or placed in the 'pentagon' position (see: **Basic Arm Positions**, *Figure 17*). On the up-beat breathe in; contract the stomach muscles lifting the tummy and chest slightly off the floor and breathe out (*Figure 47*); back to starting position and breathe in.

*Figure 47*

**45)** Lying on the back with legs bent in parallel position, arms in a low diagonal while the feet rest flat on the floor. On the up-beat breathe in; raise the pelvis slowly off the floor building a straight diagonal line between the shoulders and knees while gradually breathing out; recover to starting position while slowly breathing in (*Figure 48*);

*Figure 48*

**46)** Sitting on the floor with bent legs in the 6th position with upright torso while the hands hold the legs below the knees and breathe in (***Figure 49***);

***Figure 49***

drop the head downwards and let the top roll back with curved spine until elbows become stretched while gradually breathing out  (***Figure 50***);

***Figure 50***

straighten the spine bit by bit from the bottom to the top while gradually breathing in and raising the head to the starting position.

**47)** Lying on the back, lift both legs with bent knees while clasping them just above the ankles with both hands and breathe in (***Figure 51***);

*Figure 51*

pull knees gently towards the shoulders allowing the buttocks to lift from the floor very slightly and breathe out (***Figure 52***);

*Figure 52*

At an advanced level one may pull on the legs with the arms to a position in which the lower legs are placed on both sides of the head (***Figure 53***).

***Figure 53***

**48)** Lying on the stomach with the legs in either $6^{th}$ or $1^{st}$ position while with the elbows bent the palms are resting on the floor at shoulder level. On the up-beat breathe in. Push the rib-cage away from the floor into a vertical position by keeping the palms on the floor and stretching the elbows while breathing out gradually; hold this position and continue breathing out; bending the elbows slowly place the rib-cage into the starting position and breathe in.

**49)** Exercise **48** executed in such a way that in the starting position the arms are in the $2^{nd}$ position. When the rib-cage is lifted off the floor the arms are also lifted and either held in the $2^{nd}$ position or (at intermediate level) lifted into the $5^{th}$.

**50)** A more advanced version of exercises **48** and **49** is to execute them in such a way that in the starting position the arms are in the $5^{th}$ position and the ribcage is lifted into the air together with the arms held in the $5^{th}$ position.

**Note:** After students have mastered all the Warm-up exercises and are ready to execute them in combined versions and at both fast and slow speed, the breathing technique should be changed accordingly, (for example: when a movement is repeated at a fast speed several times in succession it would be advisable to execute the exercise fully twice—later for four or more times—while continuously inhaling; then continue to do the movement twice as a minimum while exhaling.) According to the dancer's progress, age and intelligence this can be upgraded by performing an even higher number of exercises with longer periods of inhaling, exhaling and shallow breathing. The longer the duration of an *enchaînement*, the more thought should be given to using the most economical way of breathing in order to accompany the long succession of movements. At the beginning the student should be helped to analyse and monitor his/her breathing. Often, when tasks become more sophisticated one should experiment in trying out various possibilities. Later, the correct respiration will become automatic and raise the dancer's stamina. However, it should never be taken for granted.

# PART IV

# FLOOR BARRE

# FLOOR BARRE EXERCISES

The movements described below are based on and named after the basic barre exercises of classical ballet training although in the floor barre most of these movements should be executed not only in a turned-out position (as in classical ballet) but also in a turned-in, straight 6$^{th}$ position or parallel one. Contrary to the classical barre counterparts, some of these exercises may be executed with both legs working simultaneously. In some specific cases many of these images look quite unlike their classical 'relations' but, as they are just variations of the original movements and they work on the same muscles, joints, etc. (though often differently) it seems logical to register them under the same name.

In turned-out exercises the starting position will be described always with flexed feet (as if standing on the floor in a certain classical position). While the working leg is performing the given exercise the other leg must be kept turned-out and motionless. This control is not easy (particularly when working in *à la seconde* positions). Consequently it often results in working with an uncontrolled, wobbly pelvis (**Figure 54**).

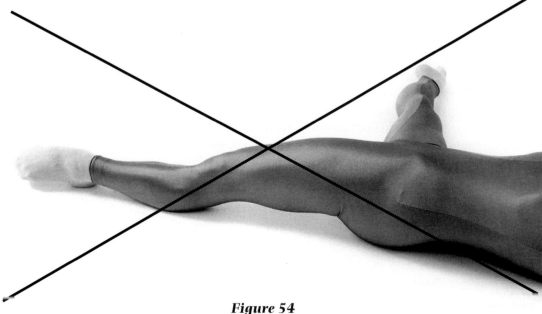

*Figure 54*

Exercising in an unstable position and an incorrect posture will hardly improve a dancer's technique and control. This common fault can be overcome to some extent by 'locking' the passive (equivalent of 'supporting') leg's turn-out and holding the foot firmly in a flexed position (***Figure 55***).

***Figure 55***

However, to hold the foot at this angle for a relatively long time might feel tiring during the first classes and may cause some stiffness in the muscles of the lower leg. Therefore, at the initial stages it is advisable to use this flexed position of the passive ('supporting') somewhat sparingly. The best solution is alternating the working legs often as well as inserting between each turned-out exercise either a turned-in or a 6$^{th}$ position version of the same movement (where the feet are pointed or just relaxed). Gradually the muscles will become used to holding the feet in a flexed position for longer periods without causing any problems.

Improving a dancer's turn-out, the pliability of the hip joints, as well as helping leg extensions to be raised higher, are some of the goals to be achieved when practising classical exercises on the floor. However, **they should be attempted within each individual's own physical capability and must never be forced.** As far as flexibility is concerned amazing results can be obtained if the basic principles of the Floor Barre practice are taken care of within each lesson:
•     alternating the turned-out positions with the turned-in, parallel and 6$^{th}$ positions,
•     movements which demand arching of the back must be balanced with their opposite,
•     pointing of the feet must be alternated with flexing them,
•     the correct usage of respiration concerning each exercise.

In case of working with students who are physically weak from illness, injury or when starting to teach the Floor Barre to children especially, it is advisable to do the *battement tendu* exercises at first with the 'feet-against-the-wall' position while lying on the back, side and stomach (***Figures 56, 57 & 58***).

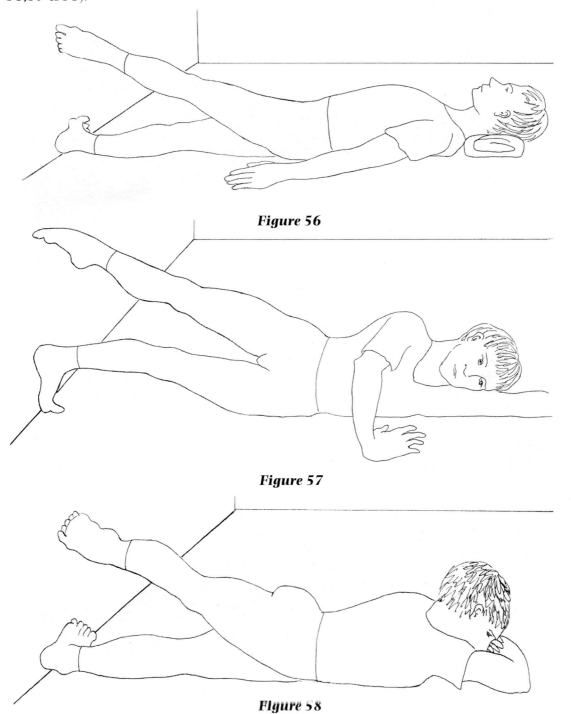

*Figure 56*

*Figure 57*

*Figure 58*

When these students have gained sufficient strength and, in case of children, enough understanding of how to control the correct placement of the whole body when working on the floor, they may practise gradually away from the wall.

## Battement tendu
### Lying on the back
**51)** Legs in 6th position with pointed feet and hands below the nape of the neck. On the up-beat breathe in; lift the right leg from the floor to a 60° angle with pointed foot (as if executing a *battement tendu en avant* in a standing position) and breathe out (**Figure 59**); keep this position and hold breath; draw the leg back to the starting position and breathe in. The same procedure with the left leg.

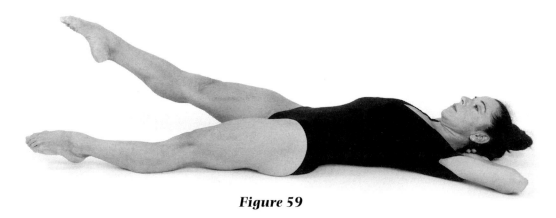

*Figure 59*

**52)** Exercise **51** from a flexed 1st position (**Figure 60**).

*Figure 60*

**53)** Legs in 6<sup>th</sup> position with pointed feet, arms in a low diagonal. On the up-beat breathe in; slide the right leg on the floor with pointed foot to the side and breathe out (***Figure 61***);

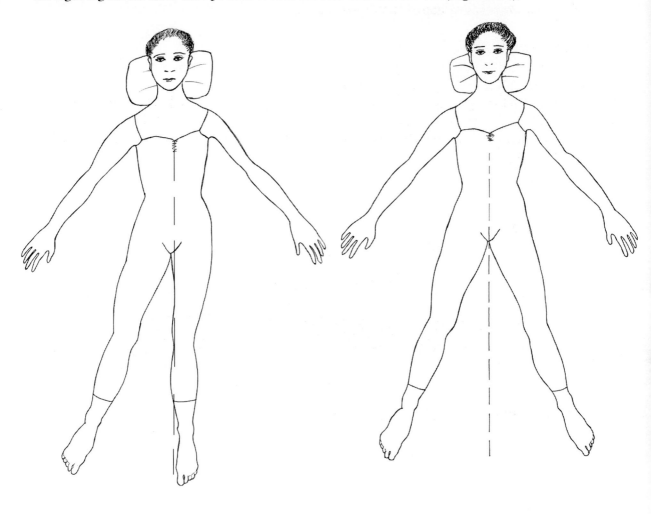

**Figure 61**                    **Figure 62**

keep this position and hold breath; draw the leg back on the floor (by using strongly the inside muscles of the thigh) while flexing both feet and breathe in. The same procedure with the left leg.

**54)** Exercise **53** with both legs at the same time (***Figure 62***).

**55)** Exercise **53** from the 1ˢᵗ position (***Figure 63***).

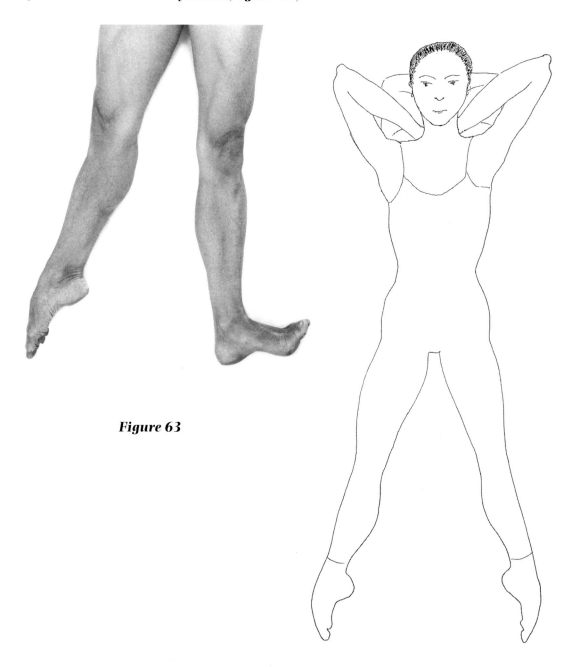

*Figure 63*

*Figure 64*

**56)** Exercise **55** with both legs at the same time (***Figure 64***).

In order to exercise and strengthen the diaphragm and abdominal muscles—so vitally important for preventing injuries—all the above-mentioned *tendu* exercises should be practised also with the head, shoulders and arms lifted off the floor (***Figure 65***).

***Figure 65***

Working in this posture helps not only to strengthen the above-mentioned muscles but it also assists students and dancers to avoid an arching of the back (especially in the initial stage of learning these exercises). The speed, rhythmical variations and frequency of use of these versions, as well as how often one alternates and combines them with those variations where head and shoulders rest on the floor, must depend on the standard, age and physical health of the student.

## Lying on the left side

**57)** On the up-beat turn out both legs into 1$^{st}$ position with pointed feet (as described and illustrated under **Basic Body Positions**) and breathe in; *battement tendu* with the right leg to the side and breathe out (***Figure 66***);

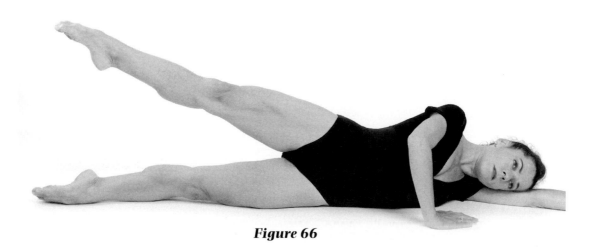

***Figure 66***

hold position and hold breath; using the inside muscle of the thigh bring back the leg to starting position and breathe in. Same procedure to the other side.

**58)** Exercise **57** executed from the 6<sup>th</sup> position and with feet pointed (***Figure 67***).

***Figure 67***

**Note:** Controlling the correct posture while working on the side is quite demanding. Therefore the *battement tendu* exercises in this position should be practised only when the student is physically strong and advanced enough to understand how to avoid faulty postures like:

- rolling back on the hip (as if sitting behind),
- arching the back (**Figure 68**),
- straining the neck (**Figure 68**),
- dropping the shoulder forward.

*Figure 68*

## Lying on the stomach

**59)** Legs in the 6th position with pointed feet, the chin or the forehead resting on the hands (as described and illustrated on pages 33 & 34). On the up-beat breathe in; lift the right leg to the back in the air to about a 60° angle from the floor while the pelvis is kept square on the floor and start breathing out (**Figure 69**); hold this position while continue breathing out; place the leg into the starting position and breathe in. The same procedure with the left leg.

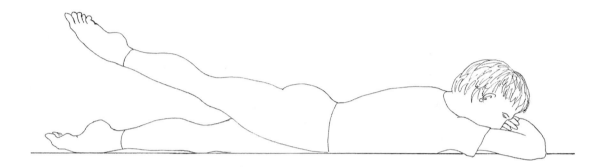

*Figure 69*

**60)** Exercise **59** with both legs at the same time.

**61)** *Battement tendu* backwards executed as in the classical ballet exercise with legs in the 1st position and feet flexed. It is essential that the working leg should never be 'over turned-out' so, in spite of the turned-out position, the pelvis is kept absolutely square on the floor (**Figure 70**);

*Figure 70*

**62)** Exercise **61** executed with both legs at the same time.

**63)** Exercise **61** executed with the arms held in 5<sup>th</sup> position on the floor and when lifting the *battement tendu* to the back with the right leg lift the left arm simultaneously in the air. (***Figure 71***) Same procedure with opposite leg and arm.

***Figure 71***                    ***Figure 72***

**64)** Exercise **63** executed with both legs and arms at the same time.

**65)** Both legs in 1<sup>st</sup> position with flexed feet, arms in 2<sup>nd</sup> position with the palms facing downwards or hands under the chin. On the up-beat breathe in; *battement tendu* to the side with the right leg and start breathing out (during this movement the hip-joint must be relaxed, the pelvis kept square and the muscles of the buttock should not be allowed to bunch up and contract but they must be kept flat (***Figure 72***); hold position and keep breathing out; draw back the leg to starting position using the inside thigh muscles while flexing the right foot and breathe in. The same procedure with the left leg.

**66)** Exercise **65** executed with both legs simultaneously.

**Note:** When the students have learnt all the basic forms of the *tendu* exercises separately and executed them in a rather slow tempo they should practise them in combined forms with various rhythms and speeds. Also, the turned-out versions should always alternate with those that are worked from the 6$^{th}$ and parallel position. At more advanced levels various *port de bras* may accompany the leg movements. To achieve better stretches and contractions in the leg muscles and more mobility in the feet it is important that all versions of the above-described *battement tendu* exercises should be executed with alternating footwork. For example: after having done in succession six evenly timed fast *battement tendus* with footwork carried out exactly as in classical ballet training (while continuously breathing out), execute two slow *battement tendus* while doing the opposite action with the foot (the *tendu* with flexed foot and the withdrawing action with pointed foot) while breathing in gradually. The possibility of variations is endless!

\* \* \* \* \*

## Passé retiré

In the Floor Barre system the *Passé retiré* exercises have in a way a more important role to play then their counterparts in the classical ballet training. By the nature of this exercise regime (practising while lying on the floor without having to bear the body-weight), movements that prepare the dancers' hip joints to function in both the extreme turn-out and turned-in positions are incomparably easier and consequently without stress. In order to enhance the mobility of the groin, these exercises—in contrast to the build up of a traditional classical barre exercise—should be performed repeatedly at each lesson in great numbers and before any turned out *demi plié* and *grand plié* exercises.

### Lying on the back

**67)** Legs in the 6$^{th}$ position with flexed feet, hands behind the nape of the neck. On the up-beat breathe in and point both feet. Bend the right knee to the extent that the pointed foot reaches the level of the left knee (only the big toe should touch the floor) and start breathing out gradually (**Figure 73**); hold position while continuing to breathe out; slide the right leg back to starting position on the heel of the flexed foot and breathe in. Same procedure with the left leg.

***Figure 73***

**68)** Legs in the 1ˢᵗ position with flexed feet, arms either in the 2ⁿᵈ position or in a low diagonal. On the up-beat breathe in and point the right foot. Pull the bent and turned-out leg into a *passé* position as in classical ballet technique and breathe out (**Figure 74**); return right leg to the starting position and breathe in. Same procedure with the left leg.

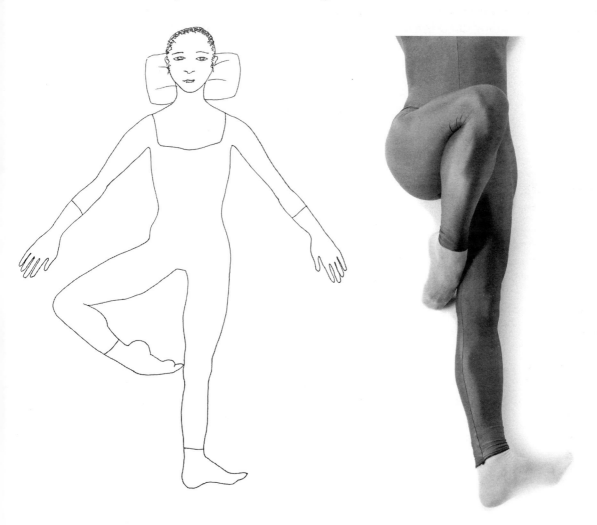

**Figure 74**                                              **Figure 75**

**69)** Legs in 6ᵗʰ position with pointed feet, arms in the 2ⁿᵈ position. On the up-beat start breathing in; *passé* in the 6ᵗʰ position (as described in exercise **64**) and continue breathing in; turn the working leg in as far as the groin allows without moving the pelvis and breathe out (**Figure 75**); recover the left leg to a 6ᵗʰ position *passé* with pointed foot and breathe in; turn out the right leg to a *passé* with pointed foot in the 1ˢᵗ position while turning out the left leg as well with a flexed foot and breathe out; recover the right leg into a *passé* in the 6ᵗʰ position while turning the left leg also into a 6ᵗʰ position with both feet pointing and start breathing in; stretch the right leg into the starting position and keep breathing in. The same procedure with the left leg.

**70)** Exercise **69** executed from a 2$^{nd}$ position with both legs at the same time. (This exercise should be used only at an intermediate or advanced level, and even then, **neither the turned-out nor the turned-in positions must ever be forced beyond the individual's physical capability.**)

**71)** Legs and arms in the 2$^{nd}$ position. On the up-beat breathe in. P*assé* with the right leg turned-out and start breathing out (*Figure76*);

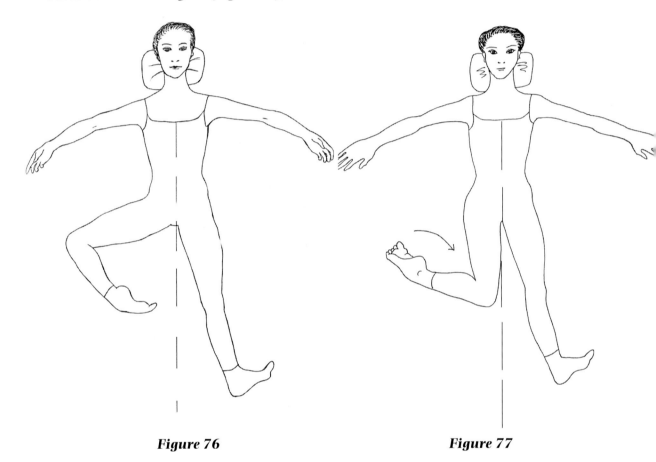

**Figure 76**                                         **Figure 77**

while placing the right foot in a parallel position on the floor lift the bent knee and breathe in; turn in the right leg and while sliding it a bit further away from the left leg place the turned-in leg on the floor and start breathing out gradually (*Figure 77*);

keep the position while continuing to breath out; place the bent right leg into parallel position while placing the right foot flat on the floor and breathe in; turn out the bent leg and place it on the floor while breathing out (as in *Figure 76*); stretch the right leg into the starting position and breathe in. Same procedure with the left leg.

**Note:** Placing the knee onto the floor when it is in the turned-out and/or the turned-in *passé* position (as in *Figures 76 & 77*) **must not be forced** in case some might find that they cannot execute them without discomfort or a pull in the working leg's groin and/or the knee joint. These individuals should practise this exercise with turning in and/or turning out their bent legs only so far as they can manage without any discomfort.

**72)** (Circling the *passé en dedans*): Legs with flexed feet in the 1ˢᵗ position, arms in the low diagonal. On the up-beat start breathing in. *Passé* with the right leg and continue breathing in; lift the bent leg from the floor to a parallel position while trying to get the bent knee as close as possible to the chest and start to breathe out gradually (***Figure 78***);

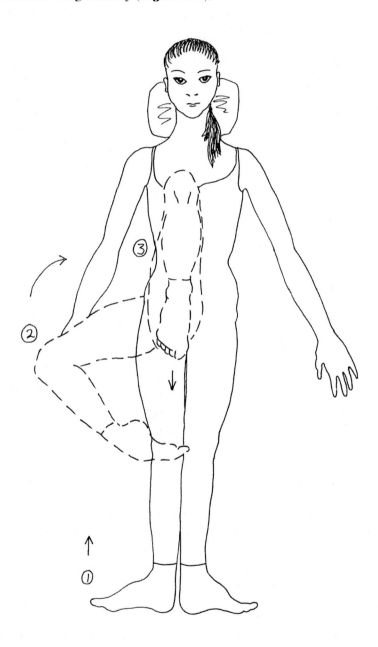

***Figure 78***

turn in the bent leg allowing the right hip to lift off the floor (facing with the pelvis to the left) while breathing in (**Figure 79**);

**Figure 79**

place the bent right knee on the floor across the left leg while trying to keep both shoulders on the floor and breathe out gradually; with the left hand hold on to the right thigh and pull the right leg gently on the floor towards the left side pointing the left (supporting) foot as well while continuing to breath out (**Figure 80**);

**Figure 80**

(circling the *passé en dehors*): Unfold the left arm and breathe in; and start lifting and turning the bent right leg towards the parallel position while pushing the right knee towards the chest and start breathing out; place bent right leg into a turned-out *passé retiré* position and while flexing the left foot continue to breathe out; stretch the right leg into the starting 1ˢᵗ position with flexed feet and breathe in. The same procedure with the left leg.

## Lying on the side

**73)** Lying on the left side in a 6th position. On the up-beat bend the left knee slightly with the lower leg behind the body and breathe in. Bend the right knee and pull it towards the chest with pointed foot and breathe out (***Figure 81***); stretch the knee and place right leg in the starting position and breathe in. Same on the other side and leg.

***Figure 81***

**74)** Lying on the left side with the legs in 1st position and the feet pointed. On the up-beat breathe in. Place the right leg into a turned-out 1st position *passé* and breathe out (***Figure 82***); stretch the leg and place it into starting position and breathe in. Same procedure on the other side.

***Figure 82***

**75)** Alternate the 1st position *passé* (while breathing out) with the 6th position version in succession.

**Note:** Dancers and students, in order to achieve a better turn-out but lacking control and strength in their torso, often get into faulty postures when practising the turned-out versions of the *passé retiré* exercises while lying on the side. The most common faults are:

- arching the back (**Figure 83**),
- dropping the weightless shoulder forward (**Figure 83**),
- straining their hands and fingers by putting weight only on their fingers and fingertips (**Figure 83**).

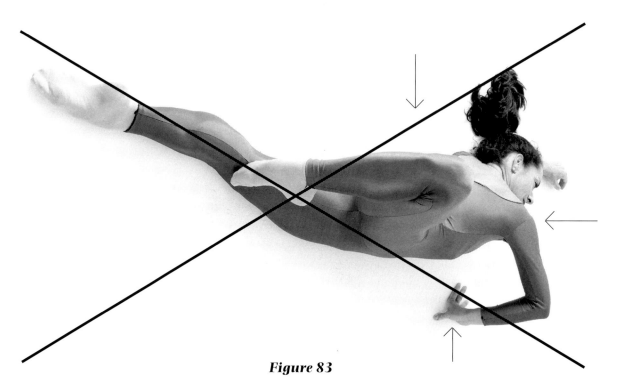

***Figure 83***

These faults must be corrected before the faulty posture becomes habitual and likely to affect badly the more intricate exercises practised on the side (*Développés, grand battements, ronds de jambes, etc.*) Such malpractice is bound to lead to injury sooner or later.

### Lying on the stomach

**76)** Legs in 1ˢᵗ position with flexed feet while arms either in the 2ⁿᵈ or the 'pentagon' position. On the up-beat breathe in and point the right foot; by sliding the bent right leg on the floor place it into a *passé* position and start breathing out (***Figure 84***); keep position and continue breathing out; slide the leg into starting position with pointed foot and start breathing in; flex foot and hold breath. Same with the left leg.

**Note:** Executing the *passé retiré* exercise while lying on the stomach seems rather a simple task but often—at the beginning stages—dancers are inclined to execute it incorrectly by bunching the buttock muscles and/or lifting the hip-bone slightly off the floor on the side of the working leg. Great care must be taken to make sure the buttock muscles are flat (***Figure 84***) so that they don't become overdeveloped and heavy looking.

***Figure 84***

For the same reasons as described previously in the *Battement tendu* exercises all these versions of the *passé retiré* exercises should be practised also with the head, arms and shoulders lifted in the air.

\* \* \* \* \*

## *Demi & grand pliés*

Whilst many exercises of the floor barre can be carried out not only in a lying posture but also in a sitting position, it is most important that all types of turned-out *demi & grand plié* exercises should be practised in lying postures only. In those cases when a dancer is suffering temporarily from some specific ailments (like having a painful scar after a back or tummy operation, infected or burnt skin on the back, tummy or side and so on) the *demi & grand plié* exercises either must be avoided or practised only in a reclining posture.

One often sees students and dancers trying to warm-up by themselves sitting on the floor practising an exercise in a turned-out '*grand plié*-like' position, holding their **'sickling'** feet together with their hands while they keep 'bouncing' their knees towards the floor, either leaning with their torso forward or bending with a curved spine above their bent legs. Unfortunately, when they do this exercise they don't realise that instead of enhancing their turn-out they are harming themselves. If practised regularly this exercise becomes not only counterproductive but it can lead to serious problems like:

- Holding the feet in a 'sickled' position while pushing them against the floor when lifting the bent knees and dropping the weight of the legs and the torso on them when bouncing the knees towards the floor is bound to over-stretch the tendons running along the outside of the feet and around the ankles. This weakens the ankles and makes the dancers prone to the most common injuries (such as sprains or dislocations).

- When turning the legs out in a sitting posture the hip joints become bent and locked in a 90° angle (instead of being completely opened at 180° as they are when lying or standing on the floor). Consequently, whilst executing the above-mentioned exercise, the turned out and bent groins become under pressure from the weight of the either forward leaning or the bent torso. At the same time the buttock muscles—which should be free to help control a dancer's turn-out—are handicapped by being flattened and pressed against the floor by the weight of the torso. So, the tendons, ligaments, muscles and joints work and react in just the opposite way from that needed to achieve a better and natural turn-out.

## Lying on the back

**77)** Legs in 6ᵗʰ position with pointed feet, arms in a low diagonal with palm turned towards the floor. On the up-beat breathe in. Bend knees slowly to a 45° angle while pointing feet (only the big toes should touch the floor) and start breathing out (***Figure 85***); hold position and continue breathing out; stretch knees slowly and flex feet while starting to breathe in; keep the position and continue breathing in.

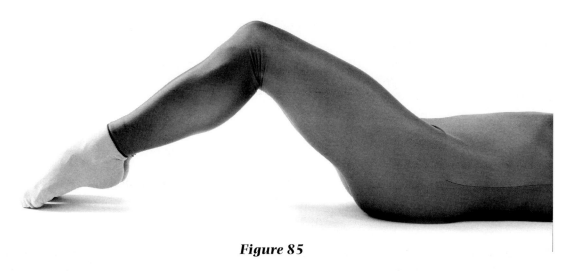

*Figure 85*

**78)** Exercise **77** executed with flexed feet in such a way that only the heels are touching the floor when bending the knees (***Figure 86***).

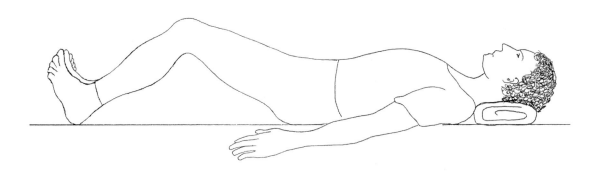

*Figure 86*

**79)** Legs in the 1st position with flexed feet while hands are below the nape of the neck. On the up-beat breathe in and point feet. Bend both knees to a 45° angle slowly drawing them towards the torso creating a diamond shape with the feet and legs while starting to breathe out (**Figure 87**); hold this position and continue breathing out; slowly stretch the knees sliding them to the starting position and begin breathing in; flex the feet and continue breathing in.

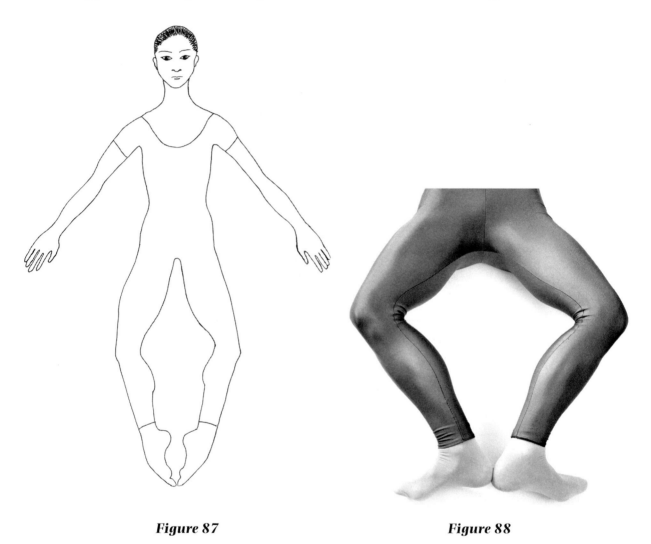

*Figure 87*                    *Figure 88*

**80)** Exercise **79** executed with keeping the feet flexed while bending the legs (as in classical ballet, a *demi plié* in the 1ˢᵗ position **Figure 88**).

**81)** Legs in 6ᵗʰ position with pointed feet. On the up-beat start to breathe in gradually; bend knees to 45° while pointing the feet and continue breathing in: open bent legs into 1ˢᵗ position while flexing the feet and breathe out gradually; keep position and continue breathing out; close legs into 6ᵗʰ position with pointed feet and stretch knees while gradually breathing in.

**82)** Legs in the 1ˢᵗ position while the arms are in the 2ⁿᵈ position with the palm turned towards the floor. On the up-beat point both feet and start breathing in. Bend both knees towards a 60° angle (equivalent of the degree of a *grand plié* in classical ballet training) while the feet are pointed and start breathing out (great care must be taken that the feet are **not sickled!**); hold this position and continue breathing out; slowly stretch legs into the starting position and breathe in.

**83)** Exercise **82** in the 6th position.

**84)** Legs in the 1ˢᵗ position with the feet flexed while arms are in the 2ⁿᵈ position. On the up-beat breathe in. Bend both legs slowly towards the 60° angle while the feet are neither pointing nor flexing but keep the heels together in the *demi pointe* position as if in a classical barre exercise doing a *grand plié* in the 1ˢᵗ position (**Figure 89**) and start breathing out; hold this position while continue breathing out; slowly stretch both legs into the starting position and breathe in.

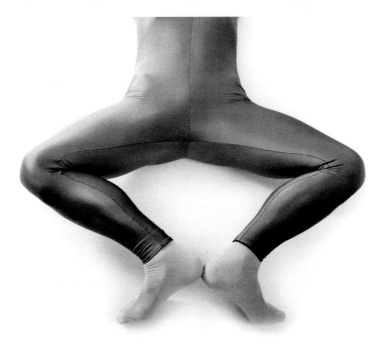

***Figure 89***

**85)** Legs in a 6ᵗʰ position with pointed feet while hands are below the nape of the neck. On the up-beat breathe in. Bend and draw the legs close towards the buttocks and start breathing out; turn out both legs with feet in the *demi pointe* position to a *grand plié* while continuing to breathe out; close knees into a 6ᵗʰ position and start breathing in; turn out legs again and start breathing out; hold this position and continue breathing out; stretch legs and through a 1st position with flexed feet turn them into the starting 6ᵗʰ position with pointed feet and start breathing in.

**86)** All the *demi* and *grand plié* exercises described above should be executed also in the parallel position as well as in the 2ⁿᵈ positions.

**Note:** For similar reasons to those mentioned previously in the *battement tendu* exercises all the above variations of *demi* and *grand plié* movements may be practiced with the head, arms and shoulders lifted in the air.

## Lying on the stomach

The following exercises may prove to be difficult for some people. Therefore, they must be practised at the beginning with great care and consideration for the individual's body-structure. They should be learnt little by little and repeated only a few times at each lesson. The *plié* exercises executed on the stomach need to be learnt not so much for their own sake but for use in later studies as a starting and finishing position in connection with some other exercise groups, like irregular *rond de jambe, développé à la seconde,* etc.

**87)** Legs in 1ˢᵗ position with pointed feet while arms are in the 'pentagon' position. On the up-beat breathe in; bend both knees to 45° while keeping the pelvis flat on the floor (***Figure 90***) and breathe out; keep the position and hold breath; stretch both legs into the starting position and breathe in; rest in this position and hold breath.

*Figure 90*

**Note:** At the beginning of these studies some pupils may find this exercise difficult to perform while keeping the correct posture and may arch their back and/or bunch up the buttock muscles. This should be avoided by allowing them to lift slightly the lower legs off the floor while doing the *demi-plié* movement (***Figure 91***). This will help them to keep the rest of the body in the correct posture.

*Figure 91*

In order to achieve the right result one can also try to execute this exercise by moving first only the right leg into the above-described *demi plié* position while breathing out; when this movement is correctly placed then breathe in; join the left leg to the right one and start to breathe out; hold this position and continue breathing out; stretch both legs into the starting position and breathe in. Breaking the movement into two phases gives the dancer the opportunity to exhale twice on the hardest part of the action, which helps them to relax those muscles which were hindering them before in executing a properly placed *demi plié* position without stress.

However, **the *pliés* to be executed on the stomach should not be practised by those students who find even these versions too stressful.**

**88)** Legs in the 1st position, hands under the chin. On the up-beat flex feet and breathe in. Bend both knees slowly to a 45° angle and start breathing out (***Figure 92***); hold this position and continue breathing out; stretch legs into the starting position and breathe in.

*Figure 92*

**Note:** Dancers capable of executing exercises **87** and **88** without difficulty and with full control should also practise the same with bending the legs into a 60° angle with flexed feet (the equivalent of a grand-*plié* in the classical technique) in the 1ˢᵗ and also in the 2ⁿᵈ positions (***Figures 93 & 94***).

*Figure 93*                                          *Figure 94*

**Note:** The correct breathing routine described so far for each Floor Barre exercise is suggested for being helpful and, most of time, identical with its counterpart in classical ballet practice. However, in the case of the *demi & grand plié* exercises executed while lying on the floor, this principle is just the opposite.

In classical ballet training a sensible breathing routine is to breathe in when performing the *plié* (this action helps the dancer to keep weight off the turned-out ankles, knees and hip-joints as well as holding the pulled up torso) and breathe out when stretching the legs. In the floor barre the dancer should breathe out gradually each time when bending the knees and breathe in when stretching the legs. The reason behind this is that when lying on the floor dancers are in a posture where problems that stem from putting pressure on weight-bearing and turned-out leg-joints do not exist, so they can concentrate their energy in the much-desired turn-out of their groins. Experience shows that the action of exhaling relaxes the body. Consequently, if the above-mentioned *pliés* are practised while exhaling, the hip-joints will become more pliable and without injury.

Later, in those cases where there is no restriction in the leg joints, one should change the breathing routine gradually, inhaling when bending the knees and exhaling when stretching the legs.

\* \* \* \* \*

## *Demi-rond de jambe*
### Lying on the back

**89)** (*En dehors demi-rond de jambe par terre*) Legs in 1st position with flexed feet, arms in 2nd position with the palms facing the floor. On the up-beat breathe in. Lift the right leg with pointed foot off the floor into a forward *battement tendu* 4th position and start to breathe out; with a semi-circle *en dehors* place the right leg on the floor to the 2nd position and continue breathing out; by brushing the outside of the right leg against the floor withdraw it to the 1st position while flexing the right foot and breathe in (**Figure 95**). The same with the left leg.

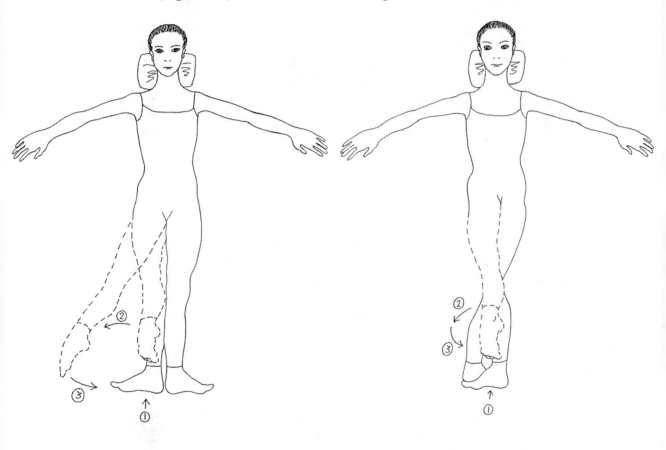

**Figure 95**                                        **Figure 96**

**90)** (*En dedans demi-rond de jambe par terre*) Legs in 1st position with flexed feet, arms in 2nd position with the palms resting on the floor. On the up-beat breathe in. *Battement tendu* with the right leg to the side while pointing the right foot and start breathing out; lift the right leg in a semi-circle *en dedans* towards the 4th position with pointed foot and continue breathing out; withdraw the right leg into starting position while flexing the foot and breathe in. Same procedure with the left leg.

**91)** *En l'air* version of exercises **89** and **90**. These movements are executed from the 5th position keeping all the *demi-rond de jambes* in the air (**Figure 96**).

The *ronds* are smaller and faster then the *par terre* versions. Consequently the breathing has to be altered (for example breathe out while doing four *en dehors ronds de jambes*, execute now four *en dedans* movements while gradually breathing in).

**92)** Exercises **89** and **90** executed from the 6ᵗʰ position with pointed feet (keeping the working and the supporting foot pointed all the time).

**93)** Exercises **89** and **90** executed with both legs at the same time (**Figure 97**).

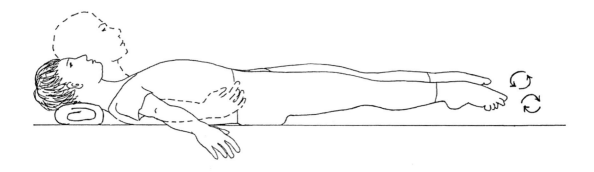

***Figure 97***

**Note:** When practising the *demi-rond de jambe* exercises with both legs the abdominal muscles become strongly involved. Most students who lack strength in this area of the torso may try to compensate for this shortcoming by performing these exercises with an arched back and strained neck. To avoid such faulty reaction—and the likelihood of later injuries—one should practise these versions only at a more advanced level combined with lifting the head, shoulders and arms off the floor at certain intervals. For example: during the execution of three *demi-ronds de jambes en dehors* keep the head, shoulders and the arms in the air but during the fourth *demi-rond* place them on the floor; then repeat this *enchaînement en dedans*.

One must take care that while executing all the above versions of the *demi-rond de jambe par terre* and *en l'air exercises* the whole torso is kept square and motionless. Therefore in the beginning it is advisable to execute all versions at a slow pace and only perform them faster when the dancer is able to control the correct placement.

## Lying on the stomach

**94)** (*En dehors demi-rond de jambe par terre*) Legs in the 1ˢᵗ position with flexed feet, either the forehead or the chin resting on the hands. On the up-beat breathe in. slide the right leg on the floor with a *battement tendu* to the side with pointed right foot and start breathing out; lift right leg off the floor circling it *en dehors* into the 4ᵗʰ position and continue breathing out; withdraw the right leg to the starting position and breathe in (**Figure 98**). Same procedure with the left leg.

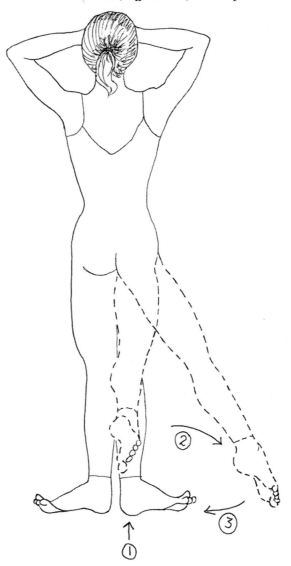

**Figure 98**

**95)** (*En dedans demi-rond de jambe par terre*) Legs in the 1ˢᵗ position with feet flexed. On the up-beat breathe in. Lift the right leg with pointed foot into a 4ᵗʰ position and start to breathe out; circle the right leg *en dedans* and place it onto the floor in the 2ⁿᵈ position with pointed foot and continue breathing out; withdraw the right leg into the starting position while flexing the right foot and breathe in. Same for the left leg.

**96)** Exercise **94** and **95** executed with both legs simultaneously.

**97)** *En l'air* versions of exercises **94** and **95** starting from the 5ᵗʰ position. All the *demi-ronds de jambes* practised to the back are kept off the ground all the time. These movements are smaller and faster than the *par terre* versions so the breathing has to be altered accordingly (see the description of exercise **91**).

**98) Exercises 94** to **97** executed from the 6ᵗʰ position while keeping the feet pointed (***Figure 99***).

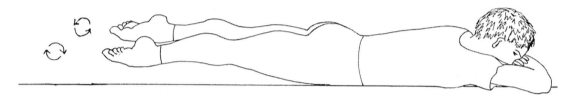

### Figure 99

**Note:** In order to achieve the required result in these *demi rond de jambe par terre* and *en l'air* exercises it is important that in the circling movements the buttock muscles and the inside muscles of the thigh (not the outside ones!) are activated. Also, for the same reasons suggested previously under the description of the *battement tendu* exercises it is important that in all the versions of the *demi rond de jambe* exercises the dancer should vary the flexing and pointing of the feet with different rhythms and accents.

\* \* \* \* \*

## *Battement fondus*

Practising the *battement fondu* exercises while lying on the floor in a 'non weight-bearing' situation is particularly useful for children and late starters. It helps them to understand how to execute correctly the sophisticated interaction between the working and supporting leg, how to control the squareness of the torso and how to breathe correctly when they are performing classical *battement fondus* in a ballet class.

By the nature of the supported posture in which the floor barre exercises are executed it will be easier for these students to put into practice the golden rule of classical ballet training: **one leg's turn-out must never be compromised for the other's sake.** It will help them to place both legs equally in a turned-out angle (which must not be forced more than the individual body-structure is capable of without stress) when the weight of the torso is not supported by the legs but by the floor. Also, in this posture it is easier to learn how to move both legs with an even and smooth quality in such specific tasks—as required in the *battement fondus* exercises of classical ballet training where the supporting leg not only holds up the body-weight but moves simultaneously with the working leg.

### Lying on the back

**99)** Legs in the 5th position with flexed feet and arms in a low diagonal or hands below the nape of the neck. Place the pointed right foot in front of the left ankle while bending the left knee (as when starting a *battement fondu* in classical ballet) and breathe in (***Figure 100***);

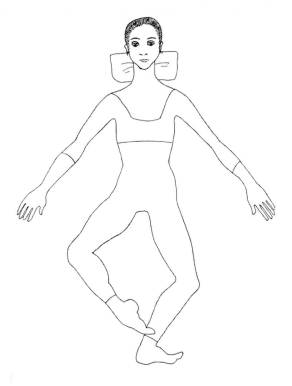

***Figure 100***

slowly move the right leg through a *petite attitude en avant* into a 4$^{th}$ position pushing the working heel forward with pointed foot and start breathing out; with a continuous legato movement stretch both legs simultaneously and while pointing the right foot arch the left foot (as if standing on ¾ point in classical ballet) and continue breathing out; withdraw the right leg slowly with resistance through a *petite attitude* position and place right foot in front of the left ankle while bending the left knee slowly with flexed foot to the starting bent position and breathe in gradually. The same procedure with the other leg.

**100)** Exercise **99** executed to the side. As the exercise starts in the 5$^{th}$ position the working leg must be stretched to the side just above the floor.

**101)** Legs in 5$^{th}$ position with flexed feet. On the up-beat breathe in. Point both feet while stretching the working leg into a 4$^{th}$ position *battement tendu* to the front and breathe out; flex feet slowly while bending both knees gradually and place the right foot flexed in front of the left ankle and breathe in. The same procedure with the other leg.

**102)** Exercise **101** executed to the side.

**103)** Exercises **101** and **102** combined with each other.

**Note:** These movements are smooth and sustained like all versions of *battement fondus*. This is specially so in exercises **101, 102** and **103** in which the working foot should move as softly as a brush stroke.

All the above described *battement fondu* exercises can be practised also with the head, shoulders and arms lifted off the floor while executing one or two *battement fondus* and then, during the next one or two *fondus* they rest on the floor.

### Lying on the stomach

All the five versions of the *battement fondus,* which are practised forwards and sideways while lying on the back, should be practised also while lying on the stomach.

**Note:** Care must be taken that the working foot must not sickle when it is placed behind the supporting leg's ankle, and that the pelvis and the rest of the torso are kept completely flat and motionless on the floor during the time when both legs move simultaneously (***Figure 101***).

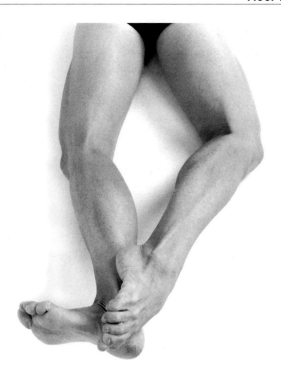

*Figure 101*

* * * * *

## *Petit battement*

From the four forms of *sur le coup de pied* positions (one *par terre* and three *en l'air*) used in the classical ballet training only the three latter versions need to be practised in the Floor Barre.
**a)** In the first *en l'air* version the flexed foot of the working leg is placed in front of (**Figure 102**) or behind the ankle of the turned-out supporting leg.

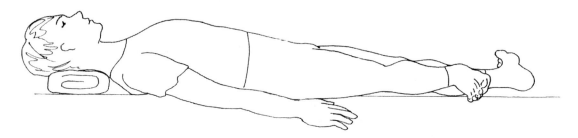

*Figure 102*

**b)** In the second *en l'air* version the pointed foot of the working leg is placed in front or behind the ankle of the turned-out supporting leg as previously illustrated and described under the *Battement Fondu* exercises (**Figures 100 & 101**).

**c)** In the third *en l'air* version the pointed foot of the working leg is 'wrapped around' the ankle in the front position (heel in front and toes behind), and in the back position only the heel of the working foot touches the outside of the ankle of the turned out supporting leg (**Figures 103 and 104**).

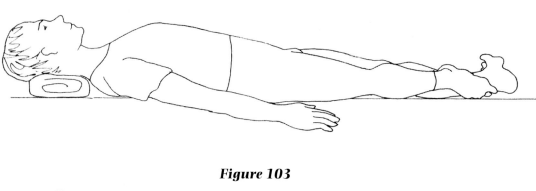

*Figure 103*

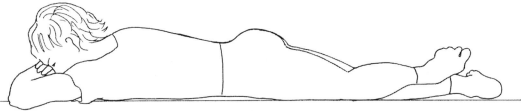

*Figure 104*

All these versions are used in the *petit battement* and *battement frappé* exercises and will be depicted on the following pages. However, these latter foot-positions do not suit people with tight joints. Though some students with fairly mobile ankle joints may manage the task as far as the 'working leg's' foot position is concerned, but their hip- and knee-joints might not be as pliable as their ankles. Consequently their bent working knee will not correctly align with their foot, which spoils the classical line and is also harmful to their leg joints. In such cases it is advisable not to force the 'wrapping round' position but rather use versions **a** and **b**.

### Lying on the back

**104)** 5$^{th}$ position with the right leg in front, both feet flexed and arms either in the 2$^{nd}$ position or both hands are placed below the nape of the neck. On the up-beat open the right leg with pointed foot into a *battement tendu* to the side (just above the floor) and breathe in. Keeping the right upper-leg in this position bend the right knee and with a fast and sharp movement beat the left leg with the right foot in the front 'wrapped around' position while starting to breathe out; open the right lower leg only so far that it is parallel with the 'supporting' left leg and continue breathing out. While performing a series of these beating and opening movements keep breathing out continuously and then, with the following series of beating and opening movements breathe in gradually, and so on... The same procedure with the left leg.

**Note:** It is recommended to practise this exercise at first at a slow tempo but later at a faster speed with the breathing routine altered accordingly. For example: while performing four fast beats and opening movements the dancer should inhale only once slowly and then, while doing the next four beats, he/she should exhale slowly. This procedure should later be extended to six, eight or more beats.

In order to strengthen the diaphragm and abdominal muscles one should practise the *petit battement* exercises in such a way that the head, shoulders and arms are lifted off the floor while doing a series of beats at a fast speed (6 or 8) and breathing out. When the next series of beats are performed rest the top of the torso on the floor while breathing in continuously.

Care must be taken that while practising any version of the *petite battement* exercises the upper-part of the working leg should be kept motionless.

### Lying on the stomach

**105)** 5$^{th}$ position with flexed feet, the right leg in the back while arms are either in the 'pentagon' position or the chin is resting on both hands. Follow the same procedure with the working leg and breathing routine as above in exercise **104** beating the right heel behind the ankle.

### Lying on the side

In the floor practice it is only possible to execute a series of *petite battements* with alternating front and back positions of the working leg when lying on the side. To achieve the perfect turned-out position of both legs—as required in classical ballet training—the dancer must turn out the stretched 'supporting' leg (on which one is lying) with either an arched or flexed foot. To balance and control the correct posture in this position (keeping turned out the leg on which one is lying whilst the other leg is executing the fast and sharp movements with a foot in the 'wrapped around' position) is rather intricate and physically challenging. It should therefore be practised at first with the support of a wall.

**106)** Lying on the left side in a 1$^{st}$ position arching or flexing both feet. On the up-beat open the right leg into a *battement tendu* to the side with pointed foot and breathe in. Bend the right knee and beat the left leg with the right foot in a front 'wrapped around' position and start breathing out; keep the right upper leg motionless and at the same time open the right lower leg with pointed foot towards the side until it is parallel with the left leg and continue breathing out (**Figure 105**);

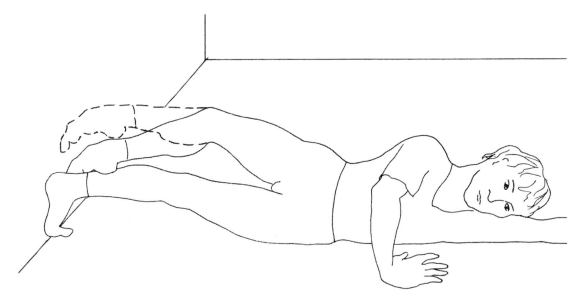

***Figure 105***

with a sharp movement beat the left leg with the right heel just above the ankle to the back and start breathing in; open the right lower leg with a sharp movement towards the side until it is parallel with the left leg and continue breathing in. The same procedure with the left leg while lying on the right side.

**Note:** After a while exercise **106** should also be performed at a very fast speed and the breathing routine should be adjusted accordingly.

At an advanced level when the dancer is capable of controlling the right posture without strain, he/she may start to execute *petit battement* exercises without the support of the wall. All variations of accents, rhythms and speed—in which these exercises are customarily performed in classical training—can be practised in the Floor Barre.

* * * * *

## *Battement frappé*
### Lying on the back

**107)** Legs in the 1st or 5th position with flexed feet while arms are in the low diagonal with the palms turned towards the floor. On the up-beat bend the right knee and place the right foot in the 'wrapped around' position in front of the  left ankle and breathe in. With an abrupt staccato movement stretch the right leg into a *battement tendu* 4th position in front (without 'snapping' the knee! *Figure 106*) and start breathing out;

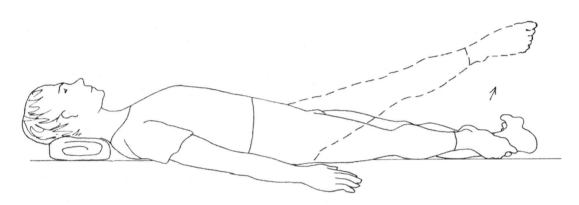

*Figure 106*

hold this position while continuing to breathe out; with a sharp movement beat the supporting leg lightly above the ankle with the working foot in the 'wrapped around' position and breathe in. The same procedure with the left leg.

**108)** Exercise **107** executed to the side into 2nd position. (Working leg just above the floor).

**109)** Exercises **107** and **108** performed with the working foot flexed when placed in front of the left ankle (*Figure 107*)

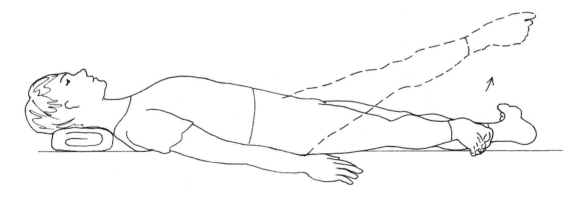

*Figure 107*

**110)** Exercises **107** and **108** executed in such a way that on the up-beat instead of beating only once the dancer performs two fast *petit battements* in front of the 'supporting' leg's ankle before the working leg stretches into the $4^{th}$ or $2^{nd}$ position.

**111)** Exercises **107, 108** and **109** executed with the working foot flexed when opening in the *tendu* position and pointing it when in the front of the left ankle.

**Note:** In order to strengthen the diaphragm and abdominal muscles one should practise at a later stage all the above mentioned *battement frappé* exercises with the head, shoulders and the arms lifted off the floor while performing a few times the *battement frappé* and breathing out gradually. Then, repeat the exercise a few times while resting the whole torso on the floor and breathing in.

## Lying on the stomach
All versions of the *battement frappé* exercises that are described in the 'lying on the back' posture should be practised in the 'lying on the stomach' position.

## Lying on the side
In order to achieve the 'balletic turn-out' when doing single and double *battement frappé* exercises while lying on the side, one must execute them in a posture where the leg on which one is lying is held in a perfectly turned-out position, either with a pointed foot (which is the easier solution) or with a arched one—as suggested above in the *petit battement* exercises. Controlling the right posture while lying on the side in these turned-out positions and performing single and double *frappés* of all kinds is fairly demanding. Therefore it is advisable to practise them at first against a wall (see under the *petit battement* exercises in **Figure 105**).

**112)** Single *frappé* to the side: lying on the left side in a $1^{st}$ position with arched feet and with toes and the ball of the foot against the wall. On the up-beat place the right foot in a front of the left ankle either in the 'wrapping around' position or by pointing the foot and breathe in. With a sharp movement open the right leg with pointing foot to a *battement tendu* in the $2^{nd}$ position and start breathing out; keep the leg in this position and continue breathing out; beat with the right foot behind the left ankle and breathe in; open the right leg with a sharp movement to the $2^{nd}$ position and start breathing out; hold this position and continue breathing out. The same procedure with the left leg while lying on the right side.

**113)** Double *frappé* to the side: exercise **112** modified in such a way that on the up-beat, while breathing in, the working foot performs two very fast *petits battements* (touching the left ankle first to the back and afterwards in front) before the working leg stretches into the $2^{nd}$ position. Reverse the double *frappé* (front, back, side). The same procedure with the left leg while lying on the right side.

**114)** Exercises **112** and **113** practised while the *petit battements* are executed with flexed foot.

**115)** Exercises **112** and **113** performed so that all the *petits battements* are done with pointed foot and the stretching of the working leg to the side with flexed foot.

**Note:** Opening the lower leg with a sharp and definite action must never be mistaken for a kind of jerky ('snappy') movement of the knee joint. Sadly, 'snapping the knee' in the *battement frappé* and *rond de jambe en l'air* exercises—a very common fault for dancers—might enhance serious injuries to the knee. This can be avoided by learning to hold the upper leg motionless during the exercises and by practising them first at a slow speed and with the support of the wall. Later, when dancers can easily control these movements and posture, they should practise away from the wall.

When exercises are performed at a fast speed the breathing routine should be changed accordingly. For example: execute two double *frappés* while breathing out gradually and then perform two others, gradually breathing in. Later this can be modified by doing a series of four *battement frappés* while gradually exhaling and further four while inhaling.

\* \* \* \* \*

## Rond de Jambe en l'air
### Lying on the side

**116)** Lying on the left side keeping the left thigh in alignment with the torso while bending the left knee slightly (see under **Basic Body Positions**). On the up-beat turn out the right leg and start breathing in. *Passé développé* to the side with the right leg and continue breathing in; *rond de jambe en dehors* (as in the classical ballet training) while breathing out; recover the *à la seconde* position and start breathing in. Same procedure when lying on the right side.

**117)** Exercise **116** executed *en dedans*.

**118)** Exercises **116** and **117** performed with double *ronds de jambes*.

## Lying on the stomach

**119)**  Irregular *rond de jambe:* Legs in a  6th position with flexed feet, while the forehead rests on the hands. On the up-beat bend the right knee lifting the right lower leg with pointed foot and with the help of the contracting hamstring muscles push the right foot as close as possible to the buttock and breathe in. While keeping thighs motionless and together start circling the right lower leg clockwise pointing with the right foot towards the direction of 3 o'clock and start breathing out; keeping the thighs together circle the right lower leg clockwise pointing towards the direction of 6 o'clock and keep breathing out; continue circling with the lower leg across the supporting leg pointing to 9 o'clock (***Figure 108***) and start breathing in; finish the circle by moving the right lower leg further clockwise pointing with the foot towards 12 o'clock and continue breathing in.

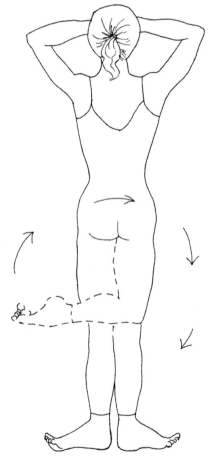

***Figure 108***

**120)** Exercise **119** executed *en dedans.*

**121)** Exercises **119** and **120** performed from the 2nd position moving both lower legs at the same time in parallel (while the right lower leg moves *en dehors* the left one is working *en dedans* and vice-versa.

**122)** Exercises **119** and **120** executed from a 1ˢᵗ position *grand plié* with both feet pointed (**Figures 109, 110 & 111**). In this version the movement of the hip-joint is also involved.

**Figure 109**    **Figure 110**    **Figure 111**

**123)** These above described exercises should be also practised in such a way that after having done one *rond de jambe en dehor,* change the direction of the lower leg by doing one *en dedans*. After each circling movement the working leg slides a little further to the side advancing towards a 90° angle.

**Note:** While exercises **119** and **120** mobilise the knee and at the same time stretch and contract the muscles of the upper leg and buttocks, exercises **121, 122** and **123** work on the same muscles and joints and additionally enhance the pliability of the hip-joints. However, the latter exercises should be practised only at a more advanced level.

\* \* \* \* \*

## *Battements développés*

In the *battement développé* exercises depicted below a normal leg extension will be at an angle of 90°. This however must be taken just as a guide line as in the early stages some students may not be able to reach this angle without stress or distorted placement (both leading to injuries). If this is the case, they must practise the *développés* at a lower angle until their bodies become ready to do otherwise. Those dancers who find that they can achieve higher extensions without any discomfort, and are able to control the correct placement perfectly, should not be held back from doing so.

### Lying on the back

**124)** Legs in the 6th position with pointed feet while arms are in a low diagonal (or hands below the nape of the neck). On the up-beat breathe in. Bend the right leg and, whilst starting to breathe out gradually, brush the floor with the toes and the ball of the foot until they reach the level of the left knee; point feet while stretching the right leg into the air to 90° (or higher) and continue breathing out (**Figure 112**); return the stretched right leg with control to the starting position and breathe in gradually. Same procedure with the left leg.

*Figure 112*

**125)** Exercise **124** executed in such a way that while moving the working leg both feet are flexed and kept so during the rest of the exercise.

**126)** Exercises **124** and **125** executed so that after the *développé* you bend the 'working' leg and place the ball of the foot and the toes on the floor next to the left knee (6th position *passé retiré*) before it continues moving into the starting position.

**127)** Exercises **124, 125** and **126** with both legs working simultaneously (***Figure 113***).

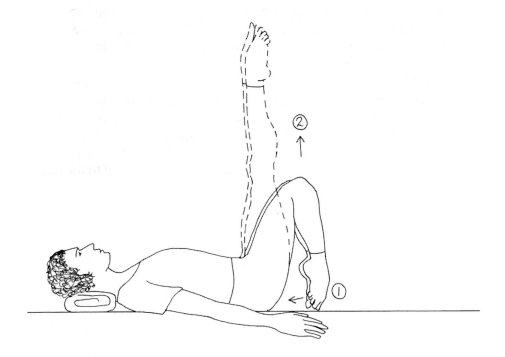

***Figure 113***

**128)** Exercises from **124** to **127** executed from the 1st or 5th position with pointed feet and turned out as in classical ballet and arms are in the 2nd position with palms turned towards the floor.

**129)** Exercises from **124** to **128** executed with flexed feet.

**130)** Exercises from **124** to **129** executed in such a way that the versions with pointed feet alternate with the flexed feet ones, as well as the versions in 6th position with the 1st or 5th position.

**131)** Legs in 1st position with flexed feet while hands are below the nape of the neck (or arms in diagonal). On the up-beat breathe in. *Passé* with the right leg with pointed foot and breathe out; turn in the bent right leg while keeping the pelvis square on the floor and breathe in; stretch the turned-in leg in the air forward across the left leg to about 60° with pointed foot and start breathing out; keep this position while continuing to breathe out (***Figure 114***);

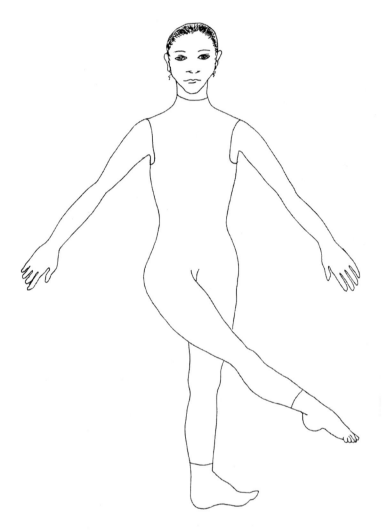

*Figure 114*

bend right knee again to a turned-in *passé* position and breathe in; turn out the *passé retiré* and place the bent and turned-out leg on the floor while breathing out; slide the right leg into the starting position with flexed foot and breathe in. Same procedure with the left leg.

**132)** Exercise **131** executed so that, when the working leg stretches forward across the left leg in a turned-in *développé*, the foot changes from pointed position into a flexed one (***Figure 115***) four times in succession and at the withdrawal of the bent leg the foot is kept in the flexed position.

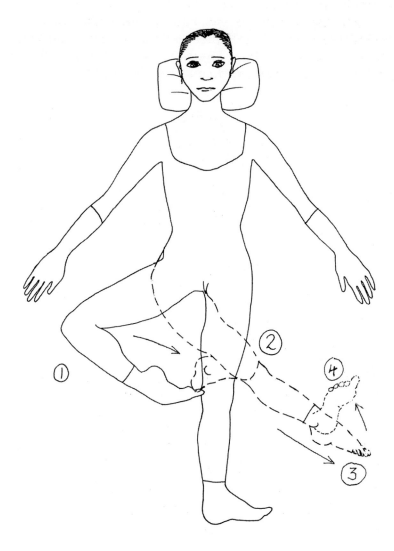

***Figure 115***

**133)** Legs in the 1ˢᵗ position with flexed feet while the arms are in 2ⁿᵈ position (or hands below the nape of the neck). On the up-beat breathe in. *Passé* in the 1ˢᵗ position with the right leg and pointed foot while starting to breathe out; *développé* to the side at an angle of 90° (or higher) with pointed foot controlling the squareness of the pelvis and continuing to breathe out; withdraw slowly the stretched right leg to starting position through a *battement tendu* in the 2ⁿᵈ position while gradually breathing in. The same procedure with the left leg.

**Note:** When a student enjoys an ideal turn-out the working leg can be placed just above the floor while it reaches 90° (or higher) as long as the pelvis is kept perfectly square. However, many dancers may find it impossible to reach this 'ideal' position without turning in the other leg and tilting the pelvis towards the working leg. This kind of compromise must not be encouraged because it will never improve the shortcoming, nor should sheer force be engaged as this is bound to lead to injury. In these cases there are two possible solutions: when the working leg unfolds to the side into the 90° either keep it so far away from the floor as the individual body structure allows without compromising the squareness of the pelvis (**Figure 116**) or unfold the working leg on the floor at a lower angle such as 60° or 80° (**Figure 117**).

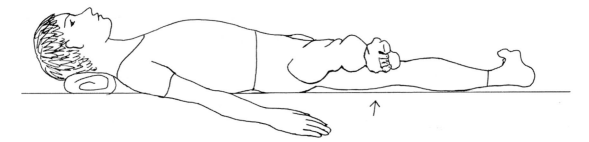

*Figure 116*

*Figure 117*

Practising this exercise regularly and observing the above detailed advice, as well as making good use of the correct respiration (breathing out and relaxing muscle tension at the moment of reaching the *développé*'s climax), will help the dancer reach a higher extension and better turn-out without harming the groin.

**134)** Exercise **133** executed in such a way that after having performed the *passé*, the foot of the unfolding leg is flexed and it is kept so during the rest of the exercise.

**135)** Exercises **133** and **134** executed so that after the working leg has reached the *à la seconde* position it returns through a *passé retiré* to the starting position.

**136)** Exercises **133**, **134** and **135** executed with both legs simultaneously.

**Note:** Naturally, in these versions even those students who possess very flexible hip-joints will reach much lower angles at the climax of the *développés* than when working with one leg only.

**137)** Legs in the 1$^{st}$ position with flexed feet while arms in 2$^{nd}$ position with the palms resting on the floor. On the up-beat breathe in. *Passé* with the right leg and breathe out; turn in the bent leg while allowing the buttock on the right side to rise just a bit in the air, and breathe in; stretch the turned-in right leg with pointed foot over the left leg while keeping both arms on the floor and breathe out gradually (**Figure 118**);

*Figure 118*

keep the legs motionless while rolling the pelvis steadily back to a square posture and continue breathing out; bend knee into a turned-in *passé* and while placing the leg in this position onto the floor breathe in; turn out the *passé* and breathe out; recover the starting position while flexing the right foot and breathe in. Same procedure with the left leg.

**138)** Exercise **137** executed in such a way that the foot of the working leg is flexing when it reaches the climax of the *développé* across the other side.

**Note:** At a later stage in these studies, and in order to enhance the stretching of the muscles in the back of the leg, all versions of these *développé* exercises can be practised in such a way that when the *développé* reaches its climax position the dancer first points the foot (while breathing in) and then flexes it (breathing out) several times in succession. At an advanced level stretching may be upgraded so that each time the dancer points the foot she/he simultaneously lifts the working leg to a slightly higher angle while breathing in, when the foot is flexed the dancer breathes out and the leg remains static.

**139)** Legs in 1st position with flexed feet, arms in the 2nd position with the palms resting on the floor. On the up-beat breathe in. Point the right foot, *passé* with the right leg and breathe out; turn in the bent leg while allowing the buttock on the right side to rise a bit and breathe in; stretch the turned-in right leg across the left thigh and breathe out; bend the right knee again in the turned-in position and breathe in; slide the turned-in leg on the floor next to the left leg and start to breathe out; stretch the right leg gradually on the floor (like an *arabesque*) and breathe in (**Figure 119**); keep this position and start breathing out;

***Figure 119***

turn out the right leg and aim to reach an *à la seconde* position at an angle of 90° (or more) on the floor and continue to breath out; withdraw the turned-out leg through a *battement tendu à la seconde* to the starting position and start breathing in. The same procedure with the left leg.

**Note:** All versions of the *développé* can be practised with the head, shoulders and arms lifted when unfolding the leg (or legs) while breathing out and when the leg (or legs) return to the starting position place the head, arms and shoulders on the floor while breathing in.

## Lying on the side

**140)** Lying on the left side bend the left knee for balance (see under **Body Positions**). On the up-beat turn out the right leg and breathe in. *Passé* in 1st position with the right leg and start breathing out; *développé* with the right leg to the side with the foot pointing and continue breathing out (**Figure 120**);

*Figure 120*

bend the right knee to *passé* position and start breathing in; stretch right leg into starting position and continue breathing in. Same procedure with the left leg.

**Note:** One must avoid arching the back or rolling on the hip backwards or forwards. Both legs must be kept in perfect alignment with the controlled straight torso (see under **Basic Body Positions** *Figure 4)*.

**141)** Exercise **140)** performed in such a way that after the execution of the *développé* the leg is kept straight and finishes the movement by placing the stretched leg into the starting position.

**142)** Exercises **140** and **141**practised so that after the execution of the *passé* unfold right leg with the foot flexed.

## Lying on the stomach
**143)** Legs in the 1st position with flexed feet while the chin rests on the hands or the arms are in the 2nd position with the elbows bent at 90° (see under **Basic Arm Positions**). On the up-beat breathe in. *Passé* with the right leg while the pelvis is kept square and start breathing out; *développé* with the right leg to the side with relaxed and flat buttock muscles and continue to breathe out; stay in this position and hold breath; *passé* with the right leg and start breathing in; stretch right leg into the starting position and continue breathing in. The same procedure with the left leg.

**144)** Exercise **143** after the execution of the *développé* the stretched leg is withdrawn into the starting position.

**145)** Exercises **143** and **144** done so that from the *passé* position the right leg stretches with a flexed foot into the *développé*.

**146)** Exercises **143, 144** and **145** executed with both legs simultaneously.

**Note:** At a more advanced level exercises **143** to **144** may be practised so that when reaching the climax of the *développé* the dancer starts to flex and point the foot several times in succession. In order to enhance the stretching of the muscles in the back of the leg this version can be upgraded so that every time the dancer points the feet and breathes in she/he pushes the legs on the floor to a slightly higher level, and when flexing them she/he breathes out while the legs are kept motionless at the same height.

When working with both legs simultaneously it is best to start from a 1st position *grand plié* (see under **Demi and Grand Plié** exercises). These exercises must be carried out with great care and the angle of the legs must never be forced further than the dancer's physique will allow without applying undue force. Although many dancers will find this exercise beneficial, students with tight hip-joints should not attempt these versions at all.

\* \* \* \* \*

## Attitudes (petites and grandes)
### Lying on the back

**147)** (*Petite attitude*) Legs in the 1st or 5th position with flexed feet, arms in 2nd position or hands below the nape of the neck. On the up-beat breathe in. Place the right foot into the *coup de pied* in front position and start breathing out; while pushing from the right heel forward and keeping the foot pointed carry the leg into a 45° *attitude devant* position and continue breathing out; stretch the right leg into a *battement tendu* 4th position and start breathing in; draw the right leg into the 1st or 5th position with flexed foot and continue to breathe in. Same with the left leg.

**148)** Legs in the 1st or 5th position with flexed feet, arms in 2nd or in the low diagonal position. On the up-beat breathe in. Place the right foot into the *coup de pied* position and start breathing out; while pushing from the right heel forward carry the right leg into a 45° *attitude devant* position and continue breathing out; stretch the right leg upright into a *battement tendu devant* with flexed right foot and start to breathe in; withdraw the leg into the starting *petite attitude* position while pushing with the right heel forward and keeping the foot pointed, continue to breathe in; stretch the right leg with flexed foot and breathe out; withdraw the leg into the starting position and breath in. Do the same with the left leg.

**149)** Exercises **147** and **148** done in such a way that after carrying out the turned-out version of the *attitude* the dancer immediately turns in from the hip-joint the *attitude* leg and then does the turned-out version again before placing the leg into the starting position.

**150)** Exercises **147** and **148** performed so that while doing the *attitude* movement the dancer lifts his/her torso into a sitting position accompanied by any chosen classical *port de bras*. Great care must be taken that when the dancer lifts the body towards the *attitude* leg the neck is not strained and is placed in alignment with the rest of the perfectly straight spine, the chest is lifted and the shoulder blades are pulled down accordingly (**Figure 121**).

***Figure 121***

**151)** All the above exercises should be practised also in such a way that instead of the *coup de pied* position, the working leg is placed into the *passé retiré* from which the working leg enfolds into a *grand attitude* and this is followed by stretching the working leg also into a 90° angle.

**152)** All versions of *grand attitude* performed with both legs working simultaneously.

**Note:** In order to involve the abdomen muscles it is advisable to perform all versions of the *petite attitude* at an advanced level with both legs working simultaneously while lifting the head, shoulders and arms in the air.

## Lying on the side

The following exercises described below (**153** to **156**) should be practised only at a more advanced stage as executing them in this position in both *attitude devant* and *derrière* demands considerable physical strength and control.

**153)** Lying on the left side, on the up-beat turn out the right leg and breathe in. Bend the right leg into a *coup de pied devant* position and start breathing out; pushing with the right heel forward and pointing the foot carry the right leg into a *petite attitude devant* (45°) position and continue breathing out; hold the *attitude* and breathe in; while pushing with the right heel forward withdraw the leg into the *coup de pied* position and start breathing out; stretch the right leg into the starting position and continue breathing out; rest at the starting position and breathe in. The same for the other side.

**154)** Exercise **153** executed to the back (***Figure 122***).

**155)** Exercise **154** performed from *passé retiré* into a *grand attitude* to the front position (***Figure 123***).

**Figure 122**          **Figure 123**

**156)** Exercise **154** started from a *passé retiré* into a *grand attitude* position to the back.

## Lying on the stomach

**157)** Legs in 1<sup>st</sup> position with flexed feet, arms either in the 2<sup>nd</sup> position or hands under the forehead. On the up-beat place the right foot into 5<sup>th</sup> *coup de pied derrière* position while keeping the pelvis completely square and breathe in; lift the right leg in the air into an *attitude derrière* position while keeping pelvis square and breathe out (**Figure 124**);

*Figure 124*

stretch the right knee in the air in an *arabesque* position and hold breath; place the right leg into 1<sup>st</sup> position with flexed feet and start breathing in. The same procedure with the left leg.

**158)** Exercise **157** performed in such a way that during the *attitude* the top of the torso is lifted and rests its weight on the lower arms (**Figure 125**).

*Figure 125*

**159)** Exercise **154** executed in such a way that the top of the torso is not supported by the arms but both arms are lifted in the air either in the 5<sup>th</sup> or in any other classical arm position (***Figure 126***).

***Figure 126***

**160)** (Irregular *attitude*) Legs in the 1ˢᵗ or 5ᵗʰ position with flexed feet, arms in either 5ᵗʰ or in 2ⁿᵈ position. On the up-beat breathe in. Raise the right leg to a higher *attitude* so that the right hip-bone also lifts a little from the floor and start breathing out; twist the spine rolling on to the left hip while the pelvis tilts and the right leg is lowered on to the floor across the left leg in an *attitude* position and continue breathing out (***Figure 127***);

***Figure 127***

start rolling slowly back on the stomach keeping the leg in the *attitude* position and hold breath; stretch the lifted leg to *arabesque* and start breathing in; lower the right leg to the floor in the starting position and breathe in. The same procedure with the other leg.

**161)** Exercise **160** modified so that when the *attitude* leg is placed across and the toes reach the floor the left leg advances forward on the floor (like a *grand jeté attitude* split (**Figure 128**).

***Figure 128***

Arms can be kept in either the 5th position or placed in any other suitable classical position. **Note:** Exercises **160** and **161** should be practised only at a more advanced level.

**162)** (*Attitude fouetté en dedans*). **Lying  on the stomach** with arms and legs in the 5th position with the right foot placed behind. On the up-beat breathe in.  Lift the right leg in an *attitude* and start to breathe out; while keeping the *attitude* leg in the *en l'air* position slowly roll over from the stomach through the left side on to the back finishing in an *attitude en avant* position while continuing to breathe out; stretch the *attitude* leg and place it into the 5th position while breathing in. Execute the same procedure to the other side.

**163)** (*Attitude fouetté en dehors* by reversing exercise **162**). **Lying on the back** with arms and legs in the 5th position and pointing the feet. On the up-beat breathe in. Lift the right leg into an *attitude en avant* position and start breathing out; while keeping the lifted leg in an *attitude* position roll over through the left side to the stomach finishing in an *attitude en arrière* position while continuing to breathe out; stretch the lifted leg and place it in a 5ᵗʰ position in front of the left leg and breathe in. Same to the other side.

## Sitting on the floor

**164)** Legs stretched forwards in a parallel position, point both feet, arms in the 2ⁿᵈ position with palms turned towards the floor. On the up-beat breathe in and turn out both legs. Keeping the legs on the floor bend the right leg in front of you and shift the body-weight on to the outside of the right hip while starting to breathe out; bend the left leg while placing it on the floor into an *attitude* position behind the torso and shift the body-weight between the legs while twisting the slightly-arched spine bringing the left arm either forward (**Figure 129**); or raise it into the 5ᵗʰ position and the right arm backwards while starting to breathe out;

*Figure 129*

keep this position and continue breathing out; recover to the starting position and breathe in. Do the same to the other side.

\* \* \* \* \*

## *Grand Battement*

### Lying on the back

**165)** Legs in the 6th position with flexed feet while arms in a low diagonal or hands below the nape of the neck. On the up-beat breathe in. While keeping the pelvis square and the torso motionless throw the right leg through a *battement tendu* into the air reaching 90° (or more) while pointing the foot, and breathe out; passing through the *battement tendu* position return the right leg to the starting position while flexing the foot and breathe in. Same procedure with the left leg.

**166)** Exercise **165** from the 1st or 5th position (***Figure 130***).

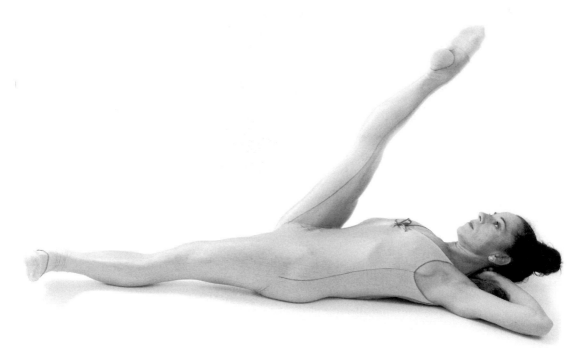

***Figure 130***

**167)** Exercise **166** performed so that the leg is thrown into an *en avant grand attitude* position.

**168)** Legs in the 1st or 5th position with flexed feet while arms in the 2nd position with palms facing the floor. On the up-beat breathe in. While keeping the pelvis square and the torso motionless throw the right leg through an *à la seconde battement tendu* to 90° (or higher) to the side (as close to the floor as possible) while pointing the right foot and breathing out (***Figure 131***); return the right leg to the starting position while flexing the right foot and breathe in.

**Figure 131**

**169)** *Grand battement retiré:* exercises **165** to **168** practised in such a way that after the *grand battement* the working leg returns through a *passé retiré* to the starting position.

**170)** *Grand battement développé:* exercises **165** to **168** performed so that the working leg is thrown into the front or side positions with a *développé* action.

**Note:** At advanced levels the *grand battement* can be carried out with the head, shoulders and arms lifted into the air.

## Lying on the side

With the exception of exercise **165** all versions of *grand battement* exercises described above should be practised also in the 'lying on the side' posture (***Figure 132***).

***Figure 132***

Although it might seem easy to do the *grands battements* in this posture great care must be taken that the dancer shouldn't be 'carried away' getting the leg to a height where the correct body posture becomes uncontrollable. As in all the exercises already described in this position (*passé retiré, battement tendu, rond de jambe en l'air, petite battement* and especially the *battement développé*, ***Figure 120***) both legs must be in perfect alignment with a straight spine and square shoulders.

## Kneeling on all fours

**171)** The *grand battement* into *grand arabesque* or *attitude* positions may be executed in an 'on all fours' posture with the elbows stretched (***Figure 133***).

*Figure 133*

**172)** Exercise **171** performed at the more advanced stage with the elbows bent and the forearms placed on the floor in front (***Figure 134***).

*Figure 134*

**173)** Exercises **171** and **172** executed in such a way that the *grand battement* starts and finishes in a *passé* position (**Figure 135**).

*Figure 135*

**174)** Exercises **171** and **172** starting and finishing in a *pointe* position (**Figure 136**).

*Figure 136*

**Note:** It is essential that while executing any versions of these *grand battement* exercises the **correct placement** (holding the torso square and motionless) **should never be sacrificed for the sake of height of the leg or a fast speed.** Also, one should practise the *grand battement* exercises in all combinations of pointed and flexed feet.

\* \* \* \* \*

## *Grand rond de jambe en l'air*
## *(en dehors and en dedans)*
### Lying on the back

**175)** Legs in the 1st or 5th position with feet flexed, arms in 2nd position. On the up-beat breathe in. *Battement développé* with the right leg in front upright and start to breathe out; circle the right leg by placing the stretched leg into an *à la seconde* position and continue breathing out; bring the stretched right leg into the starting position while flexing the right foot. Do the same with the left leg.

**176)** Exercise **175** performed in such a way that after the working leg has reached the *passé* position it enfolds only into an *attitude en avant* (90° angle) and—as in classical training when performing a *grand rond de jambe jeté*—it continues circling from this position first to the *à la seconde* and then into the starting 1st position. The same procedure with the left leg.

**177)** Exercise **175** executed so that instead of beginning the movement with a *battement développé* it starts with a stretched working leg.

**178)** All versions of the *grand rond de jambe en dehors* described above executed *en dedans*.

**179)** With the exception of exercise **176** all versions executed from the 6th position.

**Note:** All versions of the *grand rond de jambe en l'air* should be combined with more elaborate footwork of the moving leg by flexing and pointing it as well as alternating these versions from the 6th position with other turned-out ones. At an advanced level of the *grand rond de jambe* exercises the diaphragm and abdominal muscles can be involved by lifting the shoulders, head and arms off the floor.

* * * * *

## *Batteries*

In the Floor Barre system the *batteries* (*entrechats*) belong to those exercises (*battement fondu, petit battement* and *battement frappé*) which a well trained and turned-out classical dancer might not find necessary to practise unless—due to some long-lasting illness and recuperation—he/she is then unable to follow regular classical classes for a considerable period. Nevertheless, these exercises can be a great help to young students as well as those who have had a mainly contemporary training and wish or need become familiar with the classical technique and to understand the logic of these sophisticated movements.

*Batteries* are a typical example of those kinds of intricate movements that are often misinterpreted (one leg beating 'around' the other 'static' leg instead of using both legs equally, or keeping the upper legs motionless while only the lower legs are moving, or beating the heels instead of the inner legs). When practising them while sitting or lying on the floor it will become much easier to understand their mechanism and to learn how to control their presentation.

## Sitting on the floor or lying on the back

If one does these exercises in a sitting position then it is best controlled in the reclining on the elbows posture (see ***Figure 3***). If the *batterie* exercises are performed in the lying on the back position, keep arms in a low diagonal with palms turned towards the floor.

**180)** *Entrechat royale:* With the right leg in front, legs in the 5th position with feet flexed. On the up-beat start breathing in. Lift both legs just above the ground with both feet pointed into a very small 2nd position and continue breathing in; beat the inside of the thighs together into a 5th position with the right leg in front and start breathing out; open the legs into a small 2nd position and keep breathing out; while closing the 5th position with the left leg in front place both legs onto the floor with flexed feet and start breathing in. The same procedure with the left leg in front.

**181)** *Entrechat trois:* With the right leg in front, legs in the 5th position with flexed feet. On the up-beat start breathing in. Lift both legs just above the ground with both feet pointed into a small 2nd position and continue to breathe in; beat the inside of the thighs together into a 5th position with the right leg in front and start breathing out; separate the legs into a small 2nd position and hold your breath; by bending the left knee place the left foot in front of the right ankle while simultaneously lower both legs onto the floor with the right foot flexed and start breathing in. Same procedure with the left leg in front.

**Note:** On the basis of the above exercises more sophisticated *batteries* (*entrechat quatre, cinque, six*, etc.) can be also practised in the Floor Barre.

    In order to execute *entrechats* while 'lying on the back' the involvement of the diaphragm and abdominal muscles will be needed. If these are not strong enough the student might strain the neck and/or arch the back while practising these exercises. To avoid this malpractice it is advisable to do the various *batteries* at first slowly and in a reclining posture. Later it is useful to perform them lying on the back or on the stomach. One may use them to link different movement images (for example: lying on the back in the 5th position with right leg in front; execute six *grands battements* with the right leg and with an *entrechat royale* or *entrechat six* change the leg; continue the *grands battements* with the left leg, etc.).

## Lying on the stomach

All *batteries* performed 'lying on the back' can be executed whilst lying on the stomach with the help of the lower back and buttock muscles. However, when performing *entrechats* in the latter position arching of the back is unavoidable. Consequently, this should not be practised in a long series, only occasionally as a linking movement.

*  *  *  *  *

# PART V

# SAMPLE CLASSES

# SAMPLE CLASS
## BEGINNERS LEVEL

This description of a lesson is only a suggestion and an example of how to structure and build up a class for students who already have had a few lessons and learnt the specific positions used in the Floor Barre practice as well as how to perform some of the basic exercises in their simplest form and with the correct breathing.

At this phase quite a generous part of the class must be spent with exercises from the 'Warm-up' section as these movements, apart from warming-up the various parts of the body, enhance the dancers' pliability as well as having the corrective, strengthening and stretching qualities. It is important that at **every lesson** the warm-up exercises should be selected in order to mobilise and loosen up **all the main joints** of the body without fail.

As the students progress, the time given for the 'Warm-up' section within the lesson should be reduced gradually. This, however, should be achieved not by doing fewer exercises but by combining one with another and also by performing them in succession in a longer chain of movements with only a few breaks in between. (These issues will be dealt with in the description of the 'Warm-up' section and under the heading 'Note' several options are suggested.) Working in this way will not only thoroughly warm-up the dancers' muscles and raise the level of their stamina but it will also shorten the warming-up time considerably. There will be more time left within each lesson to learn and practise those exercises which belong to the specific 'Floor Barre' section.

In the beginning the exercises of the 'Floor Barre' section should be learnt with the feet against the wall whilst lying on the back or on the stomach (with the exception of the *demi-* and *grands-pliés*). Practising them in the centre of the studio should take place later when the dancer is capable of executing these movements with the correct posture. Controlling the alignment of the body when exercising in the 'lying on the side' position is quite demanding, so it is advisable not to practise these exercises before the dancers reach intermediate level.

In the descriptions of these exercises time-signatures and movement rhythms will be detailed (although they have to be looked upon just as guide lines which can be varied according to individual needs, standards and taste). As far as the correct breathing is concerned it will be taken for granted since this was discussed and described in full detail in Parts III and IV. Also it must be remembered that each lesson should be finished in a chosen resting position while slowly inhaling and exhaling quite a few times in succession.

\* \* \* \* \*

# WARM-UP section

## Hip joint

a)   **4/4. Sitting or lying on the back** in a small parallel position with pointed feet. Turn in both legs and hold position (one-and-two-and); turn them out and hold position (three-and-four-and). Do the exercise three more times at a slow speed; perform the same with slightly bent knees (or alternate the straight knee version with the bent legged one); repeat all at a faster tempo.

## Ankle & toe joints

b)   **4/4.** Sitting, reclining or lying on the back in 6th position. Point both feet and hold this position (one-and-two-and); flex both feet and hold position (three-and-four-and). Do the exercise three more times; do the same in the 1st position (or alternate the 6th position version with the 1st); repeat all at a faster tempo.

**Note:** At a later stage combine the slow part of the exercise with a neck mobilising exercise. (For example: each time when pointing the feet the head bends forwards and when the feet are flexing the head drops backwards.)

c)   **4/4. Lying on the back** with legs parallel and arms in 2nd position with palms turned towards the floor. Circle both feet *en dehors* four times slowly (one-and-two-and-three-and-four-and); do the same *en dedans;* repeat the whole *enchaînement*. Repeat all at a faster speed.

**Note:** When the students have learnt exercises **a, b** and **c** correctly they should practise them one after the other without resting in between.

d)   **3/4.** Lying on the back in 6th position. On the up-beat bend both knees and while both feet are resting on the floor draw the lower legs towards the buttocks (and). Pull upwards the arch of the feet while leaving the stretched toes and the heels on the floor (one-two-three); push the ball of each foot against the floor while lifting and curling the toes upwards (one-two-three). Do the exercise eight times at a slow speed and then repeat it faster.

## Knee & hip joint

e)   **3/4. Lying on the back** in 6th position. On the up-beat lift the right leg in such a way that the upper leg is at a 90° angle while the lower leg is held parallel with the floor and hold the lifted thigh with both hands (and). Circle the lower leg in an *en dehors* circle (one-two-three) making sure that the upper leg is as motionless as possible. Continue the exercise three more times and then do it four times *en dedans*. Repeat all and afterwards do the entire *enchaînement* with the left leg.

f)   **3/4.** Lying on the back in 6th position with pointed feet.  On the up-beat bend knees and leaving only the toes on the floor draw in the lower legs as close as possible to the buttocks (and). Stretch the right leg in the air forwards above the floor into a 45° angle with pointed foot (one-two-three) withdraw it to the bent position (one-two-three); do the exercise with a flexed right foot when stretching the knee. Repeat both movements at 60°; then repeat them at 90°; during the next three bars hold the leg in a 90° angle with flexed foot; withdraw the lower leg to the bent position touching the floor only with the pointed toes (one-two-three). Repeat the whole *enchaînement* with the left leg.

**Note:** after the students have learnt exercises **d**, **e** and **f** with precision they should practise these exercises one after the other without a break. Also, in order to stretch the ham-strings gently, at the end of this exercise (when the leg is at 90°) hold the leg with flexed foot for a longer time (for about 30 seconds).

## Elbows & shoulders

**g)   6/8. Sitting in a wide 2ⁿᵈ** position with feet pointed and with the arms resting next to the torso. On the up-beat lift the lower-arms touching the shoulders lightly with the fingertips (and). Drop the lower arms to starting position (one-two-three); lift them again (four-five-six); repeat this exercise three more times; keeping the arms in this position  lift  shoulders (one-two-three); drop and pull them slightly down (four-five-six); repeat this three more times; while keeping the fingers on the shoulder lift the bent arms away from the torso forward and circle both shoulders *en dehors* (one-two-three-four-five-six); repeat three more times; circle both shoulders *en dedans* four times. Repeat the whole *enchaînement*.

## Neck

**h)   6/8.** Sitting in a wide 2ⁿᵈ position with the feet pointed and with the arms resting next to the torso. On the up-beat lift up the lower arms placing the fingertips lightly on the shoulders (and). Drop the head forward (one-two-three); lift it to starting position (four-five-six); drop the head backwards (one-two-three); lift it to starting position (four-five-six); repeat this exercise three more times; turn the head to the right (one-two-three); turn it *en face* (four-five-six); do this to the left (one-two-three-four-five-six); do these movements three more times; circle the head starting to the right (one-two-three-four-five-six); do the same starting to the left; repeat circling again to the right and then to the left. Repeat exercise to the other side.

**Note:** At a later stage the students should practise this *enchaînement* with the lower arms following the head-movements (when the head is moving upwards and downwards the lower arms do the same, when the head turns sideways the lower arms move like 'windscreen wipers' and when the head circles the lower arms also circle parallel to and simultaneously with the head movements). Exercises **g** and **h** should be practised one after the other without a break.

## Spine

**i)   4/4.** Sitting in a parallel position with bent knees while the feet are resting on the floor. On the up-beat place the hands on the shin just under the knees and, with bent elbows, pull the legs close towards the buttocks keeping the spine erect (and). Holding onto the legs drop the head forwards and slowly and gradually stretch the elbows while curving the spine backwards (one-and-two-and-three-and-four-and); slowly bend the elbows and bit by bit pull the torso towards the upper legs while building up the spine to a perfectly straight line and lifting the head (one-and-two-and-three-and-four-and); do the exercise twice more at double speed. Repeat from the beginning.

j)   **4/4.** Sitting in a wide 2$^{nd}$ position with pointed feet. On the up-beat lift both arms to a 2$^{nd}$ position turning palms downwards (and). Turn the torso a quarter towards the right with the head turning over the right shoulder while turning in and bending the left leg slightly (one-and-two-and); turn back to *en face* while turning out and stretching the left leg to the starting position (three-and four-and); do the same movements to the left; repeat the lot but this time keeping the head *en face*. Repeat this *enchaînement* several times.

k)   **4/4.** Sitting in a wide 2$^{nd}$ position with pointed feet. On the up-beat lift arms to the 5$^{th}$ position (and). Bend the torso sideways to the right (one-and-two-and); lift the torso (three-and four-and); same to the left; repeat the sideways bends to both sides.

**Note:** Later on exercises **i, j** and **k** should be executed one after another without a break.

After this Warm-up section of the lesson is finished the students should move from the centre of the studio to places where they can sit, recline or lie with their feet against the wall. They should commence the Floor Barre section in this position.

\* \* \* \* \*

# FLOOR BARRE section

## Battement tendu

1. **4/4. Lying on the back** in 6ᵗʰ position, with flexed feet against the wall while the arms are in a 2ⁿᵈ position with palms turned towards the floor. Lift the right leg while sliding the right foot on the wall into pointed position (one-and-two-and-three-and); slide it back to the starting position (four-and); repeat this three more times but when withdrawing the leg at the fourth time change the feet into a 1ˢᵗ position; continue doing the four *battements tendus* in the turned-out position. Do now seven *battements tendus* with the right leg to the side keeping the same rhythm as the previous ones; change the 1ˢᵗ position to a 6ᵗʰ position (one-and-two-and) and rest (three-and-four-and). Repeat the *enchaînement* with the left leg.

2. **4/4.** Legs in a 1ˢᵗ position with flexed feet against the wall while the arms are in the 2ⁿᵈ position with palms turned towards the floor. On the up-beat do a *battement tendu* to the side with both legs at the same time (and). By using the inside muscles of the thighs draw the legs slowly and with resistance into a 1ˢᵗ position (one-and-two-and-three-and-four); *tendu* with both legs to the side (and); do this exercise seven more times but with the last *tendu* change the parallel position; do eight tendus in the same rhythm closing them slowly and with resistance in the 6ᵗʰ position and opening to the parallel position on the up-beat.

**Note:** At a later stage these *tendus* can be practised with reversed rhythm and accents as well as in even timing. When students have mastered all the above exercises they should execute them away from the wall (*au milieu*). For building stamina and strength it is important to practise these various *tendu* exercises one after the other in succession without a break, and also, by lifting the head, shoulders and arms in the air from time to time (for example: during the execution of the slow *tendus* lift them in the air while during fast ones place them on the floor).

3. **4/4. Lying on the stomach** in a 6ᵗʰ position with feet on ¾ point against the wall while hands are placed under the forehead with palms turned towards the floor on top of each other. Do exercise 1 in this position.

4. Legs in the 1ˢᵗ position with flexed feet while hands under the forehead. Execute exercise 2 in this position.

**Note:** At a later stage do exercises 3 and 4 in succession without a break. In order to strengthen the back one can do a few slow *tendus* so that when executing the tendu the head, shoulders and arms are simultaneously lifted from the floor and placed back on to the floor when the leg closes the position. Also, execute them in the centre. After having done this version of *battements tendus* it is wise to counter-balance the contractions of the back muscles with contrasting movements. (For example: kneeling on fours; push backwards the weight of the torso towards the heels while dropping the head down and curving the spine upwards; push the weight of the torso to starting position while lifting the head and straighten the spine.)

## Passé retiré

5.   **4/4. Lying on the back** in 6th position with flexed feet against the wall and arms in a low diagonal with palms turned downwards. On the up-beat point the right foot and bend the right knee (and), draw the lower leg towards the buttock until it reaches the left knee with the big toe touching the floor (one-and-two-and); turn out both legs and while flexing the left foot place the bent right leg on the floor (three-and-four-and); lift up the knee to 6th position (five-and-six-and); turn in the right knee as far as the groin allows *without moving the pelvis* (seven-and-eight-and); lift up the knee to the 6th position (one-and-two-and); turn out the right leg and place it on the floor (three-and-four-and); lift the right knee in the 6th position (five-and-six-and); stretch the right leg and place both legs into the starting 6th position. Repeat the exercise three more times. Do the same with the left leg.

6.   **4/4. Lying on the back** in the parallel position with flexed feet against the wall while arms are in a 2nd position with palms facing the floor. Exercise 5 carried out in such a way that while making the turned-in *passé*, the working leg slides slightly away from the other leg and the whole inside of the turned-in and bent leg faces or, if it can be achieved without strain, is placed onto the floor.

**Note:** At a later stage exercises 5 and 6 should be executed in the centre and in succession without any breaks. Also, they can be practised in different rhythms and at various speeds.

7.   **4/4. Lying on the back** in 1st position with the feet flexed against the wall and arms in the 2nd position. *Passé retiré* with the right leg (one-and-two-and); lift the bent leg off the floor placing it in the parallel position and pulling the right knee close to the chest (three-and-four-and); turn in the bent leg allowing the right hip to lift from the floor (one-and-two-and); keeping both shoulders on the floor place the right knee across the left thigh and holding it with the left hand pull the right knee gently across onto the floor (three-and-four-and). Placing the left arm into the 2nd position reverse the whole exercise *en dehors*. Do the whole *enchaînement* twice more but in half the time and then do only the first part (*en dedans*) at the original slow speed. For the next thirty-two counts just leave the right knee across the left thigh on the floor while pulling it gently with the left hand and breathe normally. Do the whole exercise with the left leg.

**Note:** When the students are able to execute all the *passé retiré* exercises correctly, they should practise them in the centre and in succession without a break.

## Demi- and grand plié

8.   **4/4. Lying in the centre on the back** with legs in the 6th position and arms in the 2nd. On the up-beat flex feet (and). Bend both knees slowly to a 45° angle (one-and-two-and); stretch them (three-and-four); point the feet (and); do the same exercise but with pointed feet (one-and-two-and-three-and-four-and); *grand plié:* repeat the exercise but this time bend the knees to 90°. Do the whole exercise from the 1st position. Repeat everything once more.

9.   **4/4.** Do exercise 8 from the 5th and 2nd positions.

**Note:** Exercises **8** and **9** should be practised at a later stage so that when doing the *demi plié* and *grand plié* actions the head, arms and the shoulders are lifted in the air and with the stretching actions they are on the floor.

10. **4/4. Lying on the stomach.** Legs in 2$^{nd}$ position, arms in the pentagon position. On the up-beat flex both feet (and). Bend the right knee to a 45° angle (one-and-two-and); bend the left leg to 45° (three-and-four-and); hold this *demi plié* position (five-and-six-and) stretch both knees into starting position (seven-and-eight-and); repeat this exercise with pointed feet. Do the whole *enchaînement* at 90° as a *grand plié*.

11. **4/4.** Exercise **10** from the 1$^{st}$ position.

12. When the students are capable of performing exercises 1 and 2 correctly without arching their backs they may start practising them with both legs working simultaneously.

## Demi-rond de jambe

13. **3/4. Lying on the back** in the 6$^{th}$ position with flexed feet against the wall while both hands are placed below the nape of the neck. *Tendu en avant* with the right leg (one-and); with pointed foot circle the right leg clockwise until the leg reaches the floor (two-and); withdraw the leg to the starting position (three-and). Repeat the exercise three more times. Reverse it four times. Do the exercises with the left leg.

14. **3/4.** Exercise **13** from the 1$^{st}$ position.

15. **3/4.** Exercises **13** and **14** can be practised so that during the execution of the four *ronds de jambes* the head, shoulders and arms are raised off the floor and with the next four *ronds* they are placed back on the floor.

**Note:** At a later stage exercise **13, 14** and **15** should be executed one after the other without any break, also in the centre.

16. **3/4.** Exercises **13, 14** and **15** practised from the 5$^{th}$ position (the working leg doesn't touch the floor.)

17. **3/4. Lying on the stomach** with the arms in the 2$^{nd}$ position with palms turned towards the floor. With the exception of exercise **13**, execute all the above versions of *demi-rond de jambe* (including the one where the head, shoulders and arms are lifted in the air).

**Note:** After the dancers have performed those versions of the *demi-rond de jambe* exercises on the stomach where they raised the head, shoulders and arms off the floor it is advisable to insert an exercise from the 'Warm-up' section which will counter-balance the arching of the back. (For example; lying on the back with the legs in parallel position. Bend and lift both legs while holding them at the ankles. Pull the legs slowly towards the torso. Breathe along and stay in this position for about half a minute before repeating the movement.)

## Battement développé

**18. 4/4. Lying on the back** in the 6th position with the feet flexed against the wall and arms in a low diagonal. *Passé* with the right leg (one-and-two-and) *développé* at 90° (three-and-four-and) flex the right foot and hold this position (one-and-two-and); place the right leg onto the floor with flexed foot (three-and-four-and); execute the same exercise in the same timing, but trying to put the turned-in right leg across the left as much as the groin will allow while keeping the pelvis absolutely square; do the *développé en avant* from a 1st position at 90°; execute a *développé* to the side from the same position. Repeat this *enchaînement*. Do everything to the other side.

**19. 4/4.** 5th position with flexed feet against the wall. On the up-beat bend the right knee and point the right foot in front of the left foot (and). With pointed foot execute a *passé développé* to the side at a maximum angle of 90° (one-and-two-and); flex the right foot (three-and-four-and); with a pointed foot bend the right knee and draw the lower leg also to a *passé* position (one-and-two-and) stretch both legs into the starting 5th position (three-and-four). Repeat exercise twice more and then twice in double fast speed. Do the same with the left leg.

**Note:** When the students are able to perform these exercises correctly they should practise them in the centre.

**20. 4/4. Lying on the stomach. 4/4.** Execute exercise **19** but from a 1st position with flexed feet against the wall and with both hands under the chin.

**21. 4/4.** From a 1st position with flexed feet against the wall execute a *développé* to the side to about 60° (one-and-two-and); flex foot (three) point the foot and at the same time slide the right leg on the floor just a tiny bit to a higher angle (and) flex the foot and stay put (four); point the foot and slide the leg a bit higher (and); repeat this 'flexing, pointing and climbing' action twice more (one-and-two-and); Draw the right leg with pointing foot to *passé* in 1st position (three-and); stretch right leg and close 1st position flexed (four-and). Do the same exercise with the left leg.

**Note:** When the students can do exercises **20** and **21** with control and with the right placement they should practise these exercises in the centre.

## Rond de jambe en l'air

**22.   4/4. Lying on the stomach** in the 1st position with the feet flexed against the wall and arms in the 'pentagon' position. By bending the right knee on the up-beat lift the right lower leg with pointed foot to 90° (and). Contract the hamstring muscles and—while keeping thighs together and motionless—start circling the right lower leg in a clockwise fashion pointing towards 12 o'clock (one-and); keeping the knees together continue circling the right lower leg pointing towards 3 o'clock (two-and); continue circling with the lower leg and pointing to 6 o'clock (three-and); finish the circle by moving the right lower leg across the left knee and pointing it towards 9 o'clock (four-and); repeat this exercise three more times. Reverse the circling anti-clockwise four times. Execute all with the left lower leg.

**23.** Execute exercise **22** starting it from a $2^{nd}$ position in such a way that both lower legs are working parallel and simultaneously. So, while the right leg is working *en dehors*, the left is *en dedans* and vice versa. Perform this exercise eight times alternating the direction.

## Grand rond de jambe (en dehors)

**24.   6/4. Lying on the back** in the $5^{th}$ position with flexed feet against the wall while arms are in the $2^{nd}$ position with palms turned   towards the floor. On the up-beat bend the right knee and point the right foot placing  it in front of the middle of the left foot (and). *Passé développé* with the right leg to the front at 90° (one-and-two-and); move the right leg clockwise placing it to the side (three-and-four-and); draw the leg slowly on the floor to the starting position (five-and six). Reverse the exercise (*en dedans*); *passé développé* to the side; lift the leg to the front at 90°; place the leg in the starting position. Repeat the exercise. Do the whole *enchaînement* with the left leg.

**25. 6/4.** Exercise **24** practised so that the working leg does the whole *grand rond de jambe* without the *développé* action.

**26.** Exercises **24** and **25** executed from the $6^{th}$ position.

**27.** Alternate exercises **24**, **25** and **26**.

**Note:** When the students can perform this exercise without strain or arching the back and are able to keep their pelvis motionless they may practise this exercise in the centre.

## Petit battement

**28. 2/4. Lying on the back** in the $5^{th}$ position with flexed feet against the wall while hands are below the nape of the neck. On the up-beat open the right leg just above the floor into a *battement tendu* to the *à la seconde* position (and). With a sharp inwards movement of the right lower leg beat with the pointed foot on to the left leg just above the left ankle (one); while keeping the right upper leg motionless in the same position open the right lower leg until it is parallel with the left 'supporting' leg (and); repeat this exercise eleven more times and then open the right leg into a *battement tendu* to the *à la seconde* position (one-and-two-and) and then withdraw the leg into the starting $5^{th}$ (one-and-two). Do the same with the left leg.

**Note:** At a later stage this exercise should be practised in the centre and with the head, shoulders and arms lifted off the floor.

## Battement frappé simple (in à la seconde)

**29. 2/4. Lying on the back** in the $5^{th}$ position with flexed feet against the wall. Perform one beat with the right leg (and); stretch the right leg to the side (one), hold the leg in this position (and-two). Repeat the *frappé* three more times; execute four *frappés simples* forward to the $4^{th}$ position in the same rhythm. Repeat the whole *enchaînement* before doing it with the other leg.

**30. 2/4.** Execute two *frappés simples* to the side followed by four *petites battements*; two *battements frappés* forwards in $4^{th}$ position followed by four *petites battements*. Repeat the *enchaînement* before doing it to the other side.

**31. 2/4. Lying on the stomach** in the 5ᵗʰ position with flexed feet against the wall. All the above-described *petit battement* and *frappé* exercises should be also practised while **lying on the stomach** with either the hands placed under the chin or with the arms in a 'pentagon' position.

**Note:** At a somewhat later stage these exercises should be practised in the centre.

## Petit and grand attitude

**32. 4/4. Lying on the back** in the 5ᵗʰ position with flexed feet against the wall while the arms are in a low diagonal with palms facing the floor. On the up-beat bend the right knee and place the pointed foot in front of the left ankle (and). Keeping the right knee bent and leading the movement with the right heel carry the leg forwards into a 4ᵗʰ position into a *petit attitude* (one-and-two-and) stretch the right leg while keeping a 45° angle (three-and-four-and); bend it again into *petit attitude* (one-and-two-and); stretch the right leg and place it into the starting position (three-and-four); repeat this exercise; do it twice more but this time carry the leg through a *passé* into a 90° angle (*grand attitude*).

**33. Lying on the stomach. 4/4.** Exercise **32** but at an angle of 45° (*petite attitude*).

**34. 4/4.** Exercise 33 executed so that after the up-beat (and) the top is lifted and supported on the lower arms ('sphinx' position) and is kept in this position while the leg is working in the air.

**Note:** During this exercise the back is kept in an arching position for quite a while, so it is advisable to counter-balance it with some suitable exercise from the 'Warm-up' session (kneeling on all-fours, drop the head forwards while curving the spine; pull the weight gradually backwards and sit back on the heels while stretching the elbows; hold this position for about a half a minute).

## Grand battement

**35. 6/8. Lying on the back** in the 6ᵗʰ position with flexed feet against the wall while the arms are in a low diagonal with palms turned towards the floor. Through a *battement tendu* position throw the right leg with pointed foot forward and up at 90° while keeping the pelvis square (one-two-three); place the leg back through the *battement tendu* position into starting position with flexed foot (four-five-six); repeat exercise; then do it twice from 1ˢᵗ or 5ᵗʰ position; do the whole *enchaînement* again. Now do the exercise with the left leg.

**36. 6/8.** Legs in the 1ˢᵗ or 5ᵗʰ position with flexed feet against the wall while hands are below the nape of the neck. Throw the right leg through a *battement tendu* position to the side (as close to the floor as possible) while keeping the pelvis square) with pointed toes at 90° (one-two-three); place the leg through a *battement tendu* into the starting position (four-five-six); repeat this movement with both feet flexed (one-two-three-four-five-six). Repeat the whole exercise then do the entire exercise with the left leg.

**37. 6/8.** Execute exercises **35** and **36** one after the other without a break.

**Note:** When the students are able to do exercises **35**, **36** and **37** with a well-controlled pelvis they should practise them in the centre. At a later stage the leg might be thrown beyond the 90° angle.

# SAMPLE CLASS
## INTERMEDIATE LEVEL

At this level of the Floor Barre studies one needs to develop further the dancers' physical strength and pliability, their control over the correct posture and raise the level of their stamina. To achieve these goals the following guidelines should be regarded in the build-up of the lessons:

- learning gradually how to perform some of the floor-barre exercises in the 'lying on the side' position (like: *passé retiré, battement tendu, développé à la seconde, rond de jambe en l'air* and *grand battement)* first with the support of the wall and later without it,

- introducing new exercise groups (like: *entrechats, adages, fondus)* which demand more strength and control,

- combining and linking the newly learnt exercises with the more sophisticated versions of the previous simpler ones into somewhat longer chains of movement as well as amalgamating them with various *port de bras*—both within the Warm-up and the Floor Barre sections. These *enchaînements* with a longer duration will not only enhance the dancers' stamina and movement memory but, being loaded with more intricate versions of the basic exercises, will raise their technical skills.

Working along with these principal ideas in mind it will be evident that the more the students progress in their Floor Barre studies the number of exercises within a well-balanced Floor Barre lesson should gradually decrease while the duration and technical content of each *enchaînement* will considerably increase.

\* \* \* \* \*

# WARM-UP section

## Ankles, hip joints, spine & knees

**a)** **6/4. Sitting** in 6th position while reclining on the elbows. On the up- beat flex both feet (and). Point both feet and bend knees slightly (one-and-two-and-three-and-); flex feet and stretch knees (four-and-five-and-six-and); repeat this exercise; turn out legs (and); repeat the exercise twice in the 1st position; repeat the whole *enchaînement* twice more in such a way that when pointing the feet and bending the knees the head drops forward and when flexing the feet and stretching the knees the head goes backwards; continue for four more times so that when the head drops forward the spine curves backwards and when the head is to the back the spine straightens.

## Neck, ankles, hip joints & knees

**b)** **6/4. Sitting** in the 6th position while reclining on the elbows. On the up-beat flex feet (and-). Circle feet parallel four times (the right foot moves *en dehors*, at the same time the left does it *en dedans* (one-and-two-and-three-and-four-and-five-and-six-and) while the head circles four times in the same rhythm following the right foot's clockwise direction; repeat four times in the other direction.

**c)** **6/4. Lying on the back** in a 2nd position with flexed feet and the arms in a low diagonal. On the up-beat point feet (and). Bend both knees to a 45° angle and turn them in (one-and-two-and); lift the bent knees into parallel position while the pointed toes are still on the floor and continue the movement by turning out bent knees and place the legs on the floor with flexed feet like a 2nd position *demi plié* (three-and-four-and); stretch knees with flexed feet (five-and-six); point feet (and); repeat this exercise bending the knees at 60°; repeat twice bending the knees at 90°; reverse exercise *en dedans* four times. Repeat the whole *enchaînement* lifting the head, shoulders and arms in the air on the first four counts of each exercise (one-and-two-and-three-and-four and) and back on the floor (five-and-six-and).

**Note:** At a later stage exercises **a**, **b** and **c** should be practised in succession without a break in between.

## Neck & spine

**d)** **4/4. Sitting** in a wide 2nd position with pointed feet. On the up-beat place bent arms behind the back in such a way that the lower arms lift upwards while the hands are placed flat on top of each other between the shoulder-blades with palms turned away from the torso (and). Drop the forward-facing head over the right shoulder (one-and); lift the head into starting position (two-and); drop the head over the left shoulder (three-and); lift the head (four-and); repeat (one-and-two-and-three-and-four); keeping the left arm between the shoulder-blades lift the right arm into 5th position (and); bend the top of the torso to the left (one-and-two-and-three-and-four-and); recover and place right hand back between the shoulder-blades (one-and-two-and-three-and-four); lift the left arm into 5th position (and); bend to the right (one-and-two and-three-and-four-and); recover (one-and-two-and-three-and-four); place the left arm to the starting position (and). Repeat the whole exercise 3 times.

e) **4/4. Lying on the back** in parallel position with pointed feet. On the up-beat lift both legs bent in the air clasping the shin-bone with the hands from outside the legs (and). By bending the arms pull the legs bit by bit towards the torso and lift the head off the floor (one-and-two-and-three-and); relax the arms and place the head onto the floor (four-and); repeat the exercise a few more times.

## Spine, feet, elbow & hands

f) **4/4. Lying on the back** with the legs in parallel position with the arms placed in a low diagonal, palms turned towards the floor. On the up-beat bend both knees and pull the legs towards the torso while feet are flat on the floor (and). Lift the pelvis off the floor making a straight diagonal line between the knees and the shoulders (one-and); hold this body position and arch the feet—leaving toes and heel on the floor—at the same time lift the knuckles of the hand with fingertips and the inside of the wrist pressed against the floor (two); drop the arched feet and knuckles onto the floor and lift toes and fingers in the air (and); repeat these feet and hand contractions and releases once more (three-and) put the pelvis on the floor and rest (four-and). Repeat the exercise six or eight times.

**Note:** At a later stage exercise **d**, **e** and **f** should be performed—perhaps with less repetition—one after the other without a break.

g) **6/4. Lying on the back** in 1st position with flexed feet with arms in the 2nd position and palms turned towards the floor. On the up-beat point the right foot (and). *Passé retiré* with the right leg (one-and); lift the bent leg and pull the knee towards the chest while lifting right lower arm parallel with the right upper-leg (two-and); place the right leg across the left thigh and with the help of the left arm pull the right knee onto the floor while keeping the right shoulder and upper arm on the floor, the right lower-arm keeps moving in an *en dedans* circle (three-and); unfold the right leg and move it *en dehors* to a *passé retiré* in the 1st position while the right lower arm does an *en dehors* circle (four-and-five-and); stretch right leg and place it into the 1st position with flexed foot while right lower arm does another *en dehors* (six-and); repeat the *enchaînement* (and-one-and-two-and-three-and-four-and-five-and-six-and); repeat the first half of the exercise and instead of unfolding the right leg pull it gently with the left arm (four-and-five-and-six-and) place both arms in the 5th position and while keeping the right leg in the *passé retiré* turn via the left side on to the stomach and start breathing in (one-and-two-and-three-and); unfold the right leg into an *à la seconde* at 90° (three-and-four-and); close the right leg into 1st position with both feet pointing and breathe in (five-and) roll onto the back (six-and). Do the whole *enchaînement* to the other side.

h) **6/4. Lying on the stomach** with arms in the 5th and legs in the 1st positions with pointed feet. Elongate the right arm and the right leg by pulling out from the shoulder and hip-joint (one-and); do the same with the left arm and leg (two-and); repeat these movements twice (three-and-four-and-five-and-six-and); bend arms with the hands on top of each other and under the forehead, while contracting the stomach, diaphragm, breast and buttock muscles lift the stomach and chest off the floor (one-and-two-and-three-and); place them on the floor and rest (four-and-five-and-six-and). Execute the *enchaînement* starting with the left arm and leg. Repeat everything.

**Note:** When the dancers can execute exercises **g** and **h** correctly they should practise  them one after the other without a break. Later, they can link exercises **d**, **e**, **f**, **g** and **h**. According to the dancers' age, previous experience and musicality this chain of exercises can be executed in two different ways. In a simpler way one can change the time-signature of **g** and **h** to **4/4** and the entire *enchaînement* can be performed in the same time-signature. The more advanced version of this task is to execute the *enchaînement* without changing the original time-signatures.

# FLOOR BARRE section

## Battement tendu and demi or grand plié

All versions of the *battements tendus* learnt at the beginning stages should be combined with some *demi* and *grands pliés* in the 1st, 6th and 2nd positions. For example:

1. **2/4. Lying on the back** in the 6th position do two *tendus* forward with the right leg (one-and-two-and; one-and-two-and) slow *demi plié* in the 6th position and stretch (one-and-two-and; one-and-two-and); do this *enchaînement* from the 1st position while lifting the head, shoulders and arms in 2nd position off the floor; do the lot with the left leg. Repeat everything but each time when the *tendus* are performed from the 1st position execute them in the 5th position instead (also, when working in the 5th lift the head, shoulders and arms each time but when working in the 6th position always place them back onto the floor) and on the last beat place both legs in the 6th position; execute eight double timed *tendus* to the side with both legs simultaneously (one-and); (two-and); (one-and); (two-and); (one-and); (two-and); (one-and); (two-and); (one-and); (two-and); while lifting the head, shoulders and arms in the 2nd position off the floor perform another lot of eight *battements tendus* from the 1st to the 2nd position with both legs simultaneously; while placing the head, shoulders and arms back onto the floor execute a slow *grand plié* in the 2nd position (one-and-two-and: one-and-two-and); repeat the *grand plié* in the 2nd position.

2. **2/4.** (At the wall) **Lying on the left side** with the legs in 1st position while the toes and ball of both feet are pressed against the wall (as if standing on ¾ rise), left arm in 5th position and the right palm placed on the floor in front of the chest. Perform in this posture *battement tendus* to the side with various rhythms with pointed and flexed feet. When the dancers are able to control their posture while executing these *à la seconde tendus* they should do them in the centre without the support of the wall.

3. **2/4.** *Battement tendus* executed *en quatre*: while lying on the back execute any chosen *battement tendu enchaînement* forwards; roll onto the side and do the exercise in this position sideways; roll onto the stomach and repeat the *enchaînement* backwards; roll to the side and do the exercise again. Then do the whole *enchaînement* with the other leg.

## Passé retiré

As they progress students should learn to execute *passé retirés* while lying on the side in addition to those versions that they have learnt already while lying on the back and on the stomach. For example:

4. **6/4. Lying on the left side** in the 6th position with both feet resting against the wall with the head resting on the stretched left arm while the right arm is bent in front of the chest. Bend the right knee while pointing the foot and pull it towards the chest (one-two); stretch it into starting position (three-and); repeat it (one-two-three); turn out right leg and do a turned

out *passé* and hold the position (one-two-three-and); stretch the right leg into starting position (one-two-three); repeat the whole *enchaînement;* do seven turned-out *passé retirés;* instead of the last *passé retiré* turn into the 'lying on the back' position while placing both arms in the 5th position. Execute the whole *enchaînement* in this posture but instead of the last *passé*, roll on to the right side placing the left hand on the floor in front of the chest. Now do the entire *enchaînement* with the left leg.

**Note:** At a later stage exercise **4** should be practised without the support of the wall.

## Demi-rond de jambe

All previously learnt versions of the *demi-rond de jambe* exercises should be practised. According to individual needs, age and dance background students may be challenged by demanding from them faster variation in speed, foot work (flexing and pointing), rhythm and accompanying work with the top of the body (lifting head, shoulders and arms). In addition they should also practise *demi-ronds de jambes* executed from the 5th position. For example:

5.  **6/4. Lying on the back** with flexed feet in the 1st position while arms are either behind the nape of the neck or in a low diagonal position. On the up-beat point the right foot and execute with the right leg a *battement tendu* forward into the 4th position (and-). Place the right leg into a 2nd position to the side (one-and); using the inside thigh muscles draw the right leg with flexed foot into the 1st position (two-and-three); repeat them in such a way that the right leg finishes the *rond de jambe en dehors* in the 5th position (and-four-and-five-and-six); continue doing five fast *demi-rond de jambes en dehors* closing them always in the 5th position (and-one-and-two-and-three-and-four-and-five) close the right leg into 1st position (and-six). Repeat the *enchaînement en dedans* and while doing so lift the head, shoulders and the arms into the air. Perform the entire *enchaînement* with the other leg.

6.  **6/4.** Perform exercise **5** as described above and then repeat the whole *enchaînement* once while lifting the head, shoulders and arms in the 2nd position off the floor each time when working *en dedans*.

7.  Exercise **5** in the **lying on the stomach** position.
8.  Exercise **6** in the **lying on the stomach** position done so that when the top of the torso is lifted the arms are placed in either the 5th position or one arm in a 5th while the other is in a 2nd.

**Note:** Exercises **6** and **7** are extremely important as they use and strengthen those muscles of the back which play a vital part in performing all types of *arabesques, attitudes* and, especially, the *penché* positions in classical ballet. However, in this version the back will be arched. To avoid overstraining the back muscles, it is advisable to counter-balance this arching action. This can be achieved best by always following exercises **6** and **7** with a movement which stretches the back muscles in the opposite manner. For example: choose exercise **44** from the **Mobilising the Spine section** (*Figure 47*) and alternate it with exercise **6** or **7**.

## Battement fondu

9. **4/4. Lying on the back** with legs in the 5$^{th}$ position with flexed feet while arms are in a low diagonal. Bend both knees slowly while placing the pointed right foot in front of the left in a *coup de pied* position (one-and-two-and); stretch the right leg slowly up and forward to a 4$^{th}$ position still with pointed foot while stretching the left leg and pointing the left foot as well (three-and-four-and); do the *battement fondu* to the side (one-and-two-and-three-and-four). Repeat these movements but lift the head, shoulders and arms in the 2$^{nd}$ position. Repeat again while resting the upper torso on the floor. Do it once more but lifting the upper torso *en l'air.* Execute the entire *enchaînement* with the other leg.

10. While **lying on the stomach** execute exercise **9**.

**Note:** At a somewhat later time exercises **8** and **9** can be combined with *demi-rond de jambe en l'air* versions. Time signatures have to be adapted accordingly. For example:

11. **4/4.** After having done two *battements fondus* into the 4$^{th}$ or 2$^{nd}$ position, the working leg, instead of doing the third and fourth one, executes four *demi-ronds de jambes en l'air en dehors* or *en dedans* accordingly (each *demi-rond* in **2/4** counts).

12. Do exercise **10** in such a way that whenever the leg performs a *demi-rond de jambe* the head, shoulders and arms in 2$^{nd}$ position are lifted off the floor.

## Petit battement

13. While **lying on the side** with the legs in the 1$^{st}$ position and the toes as well as the ball of both feet pressed against the wall execute *petit battement* (as described in exercise **106**, **Figure 105**) to the front and to the back in various rhythms and accents. Later, when the dancer is ready, one should practise them in the centre without the support of the wall.

## Battement frappé (simple and double)

14. **Lying on the side** execute the different versions of *battement frappé* (see exercise **113**) while with the legs in the 1$^{st}$ position and the toes and the ball of the foot are pressed against the wall. Later, if the student's control allows it, one should practise all variations of the *frappé* in the centre.

15. **2/4. Lying on the left side** in first position with the toes and ball of the foot pressed against the wall. On the up-beat open to the side the turned-out right leg and with pointing foot (and). Perform eight *petits battements* alternating front and back (one-and-two-and + one-and-two-and); do four *frappés simples* alternating front and back (one-and-two-and + one-and-two-and). Repeat the *enchaînement* but instead of four *frappés simples* perform four *frappés doubles.* When the students have mastered this exercise with perfect stance the *enchaînement* should be performed without the support of the wall.

## Rond de jambe en l'air (simple and double at 45$^{\circ}$)

16. **2/4. 'Lying on the** left **side'** in the 1$^{st}$ position with the toes and the ball of the foot pressed

against the wall. On the up-beat place the pointed right foot in front of the left ankle (and). With the right lower leg perform a semi-circle *en dehors* stretching the right leg to the side (one-and); continue circling *en dehors* (two-and); repeat the whole movement three more times; perform four *double ronds de jambes en dehors;* perform the whole *enchaînement en dedans.* Repeat on the other side with the left leg. When the dancer can control a proper posture while doing this exercise, she/he should practise it without the support of the wall.

**17.** Combine exercise **15** (*petit battement* combined with *frappé*) with exercise **16**.

**18. 3/4.** Exercise **16** executed at 90° starting from a *passé* position. At first this movement should be practised with the support of the wall. Only when it is correctly performed should one do without the support.

## Attitude (irregular)

**19. 6/4. Lying on the stomach** with the legs and arms in 5$^{th}$ position with the right leg to the back. On the up-beat point the right foot (and). Lift the right leg either into a *petite attitude* or into a *passé* (one-and); while rolling gradually onto the left side start raising the leg into a 90° *attitude en arrière* position (two-and-three-and); while keeping the *attitude* position with the leg, place the right big toe on to the floor (four-and) hold this position while placing the right arm in the 2$^{nd}$ position (five-and-six-and); Holding the right leg in the *attitude* place the right arm slowly into 5$^{th}$ position and roll gradually onto the stomach (one-and-two-and-three-and); lower the right leg into a *petite attitude* (four-and) slowly stretch the right leg into a *petite arabesque* and place it into 1$^{st}$ position with flexed foot (five-and-six) place the left leg behind the right into a 5$^{th}$ position (and). Do the exercise with the left leg.

**20.** After practising the above exercise it is advisable to perform a few times one of the spine mobilising movements designed to counterbalance the arching of the back already familiar from the 'Warm-up' section. (For example: see exercise **46, Figure 49** and **50**).

## Adage

**21. 6/4 Lying on the back** with legs in the 6$^{th}$ position and arms in a 5$^{th}$. *Passé* with the right leg (one-and); slowly stretch the leg forwards to 90° (two-and) flex right foot (three-and); with slow control lower the leg almost to the floor (four-and-five-and); turn out both legs and close 5$^{th}$ position (six-and); repeat *développé* but this time with turned-out leg (one-and-two-and-three-and) lower the right leg with flexed foot into 5$^{th}$ position (four-and-five-and-six-and); perform a *grand rond de jambe en l'air en dehors* starting it with a *développé* but this time keep the foot pointed (one-and-two-and); circle the stretched leg and place it on the floor into a 90° second position (three-and-four-and); withdraw the right leg into starting position (five-and-six-and); execute an *en dedans grand rond de jambe* starting with a *développé à la seconde* (one-and-two-and); lift the stretched right leg off the floor with a pointed foot and with a circling movement place it in front at 90° (three-and-four-and); lower the stretched leg into the 5$^{th}$ position (five-and-six-and); while rolling onto the left side and leaving the left arm in the 5$^{th}$ position place the right palm on the floor in front of the chest and execute a *passé* (one-

and); *développé* with the right leg to the *à la seconde* into 90° (two-and); flex the right foot (three-and) lower the right leg towards a 5<sup>th</sup> position behind the left leg (four-and five-and); bend the right knee and pointing the foot place the right heel behind the left ankle (six-and); repeat the *développé* and the lowering of the leg but this time finish it in the front *coup de pied* position (one-and-two-and-three-and-four-and-five-and-six-and); repeat the *battement développé* but this time keep the right foot pointed (one-and-two-and-three-and); execute a single *rond de jambe en l'air en dehors* with the right lower leg (four-and-five-and-six-and); do a single *rond de jambe en l'air en dedans* with the right leg (one-and-two-and-three-and); lower the leg (four-and-five-and); bend the right knee and place the pointed foot behind the left ankle (six-and); *passé* with the right leg (one-and); place the right leg into an 'irregular *attitude en arrière*' position by sliding the right foot to the back with toes touching the floor (see exercise **156, *Figure 122***), (two-and-three-and); stretch right leg into an *arabesque* position (four-and) roll onto the back and while placing the arms into the 5<sup>th</sup> position slide the right leg into a 90° *à la seconde* position (four-and); lower the right leg through the 1<sup>st</sup> position (five-and); into the 6<sup>th</sup> position with pointed feet (six-and). Do the whole *enchaînement* with the left leg to the other side.

22. **6/4.** At a later stage the above *adage* can be practised in such a way that when lying on the side—instead of doing a single *rond de jambe en l'air*—one does doubles. Also, when lying on the side, one may insert a few fast *petits battements* each time the working leg is in the *coup de pied* position just before starting to unfold the *développé* to the side.

## Grand battement

23. Should be practised in the **lying on the side** position into an *à la seconde* at first with the support of the wall: in the starting position the legs are in 1<sup>st</sup> position with the toes and ball of the foot pressed against the wall (as if standing on a ¾ rise). Later, when the dancer can do this with the correct posture, one should practise these *grands battements* without the support of the wall but in such a way that the 'supporting' knee is bent and the lower leg placed on the floor behind the straight spine and upper leg. (See ***Figure 132***). At an even later stage—only when the student can perform this task with perfect control—one should practise this version of the *grand battement* from a turned-out starting position with both knees stretched and feet pointed.

24. **4/4. Lying on the back,** legs in the 6<sup>th</sup> with the feet flexed and with the arms in 5<sup>th</sup> position. On the up-beat throw the right leg with pointed foot forward into a 90° angle (and). Hold this position (one) lower the leg while turning out both legs into 5<sup>th</sup> position with flexed feet (and-two) *grand battement devant* turned out (and) lower the leg and change both legs into 6<sup>th</sup> position (three-and-four); repeat the *enchaînement* (and-one-and-two-and-three-and-four) perform six *battements tendus* to the side in parallel positions with both legs simultaneously with feet flexed (and-one-and-two-and-three-and-four, and-one-and-two); roll onto the left side with both legs turned out in 1<sup>st</sup> position with pointed feet while leaving the left arm in the 5<sup>th</sup> position and placing right palm on the floor in front of the chest (and-three-and-four); four *grands battements* to the *à la seconde* (and-one-and-two-and-three-and-four; and-one-and-two-and-three-and-four); do six *battements tendus* in the 1<sup>st</sup> position (one and two-and-three-and-

four-and, one-and-two-and); roll onto the back into the starting position (three-and-four). Execute the whole *enchaînement* with the left leg to the other side. Repeat, but this time, when in the 'lying on the back' position and the *grands battements* are performed, lift the head, shoulders and arms off the floor each time when the leg is lowered to the 6th or the 5th position and when it is thrown up to 90° then rest the whole torso and arms on the floor. Also, when the *grands battements* are executed in the 'lying on the side' position do them with flexed feet.

25. **'Kneeling on all fours'** (see exercise **171**, *Figure 133*) on the up-beat *grand battement* in *arabesque* position (and). Hold the position (one); lower the leg into the starting position (and-two); repeat the movement but this time throw the leg into an *attitude* position (and-three-and-four); repeat the whole *enchaînement*. Perform this with the left leg. Repeat all but this time the start and finish of each *grand battement* should be from the *passé* position (see exercise **173**, *Figure 135*).

**Note:** In the latter version special care must be taken on the posture of the spine. By its nature, the execution of a *grand battement en arrière* causes the centre of the back to arch. Therefore, this arching of the spine should alternate with a completely contrasting movement (like the above described *passé* version in which the forward dropped head and the rounded spine-line will counteract the arching movement).

26. For the purpose of building the dancer's stamina at a later stage exercise **24** and **25** may be linked together and practised without a break in such a way that on the end of exercise **24**, instead of rolling from the 'lying on the side' position to the 'lying on the back' position, roll from the side on to the stomach and bend both arms placing the palms in front of the shoulders (and-three); push with the palms against the floor and lift the torso parallel with the floor into a 'kneeling on all fours' position (and-four), then continue with exercise **25**.

**Note:** At a somewhat later stage these or similar *enchaînements* should be executed with the various chosen *ports de bras*.

## Entrechats (royale, quatre and six)

27.  **2/4.** Practising these exercises in the **sitting** or the **reclining** positions is only necessary if the student hasn't yet studied *batteries*. For the same reason it is also necessary for them to study these exercises at first in their simple form without combining them in any *enchaînement*. Later they may practise them in the '**lying on the back**' position and perhaps combine and link them together in a chain of movements. In order to strengthening the diaphragm and lower abdominal muscles as well as to avoid the arching of the back or/and straining of the neck when executing these *enchaînements* the head, arms and shoulders should be lifted up and held for two or four bars of **2/4** counts, and then placed back to the floor for a similar length of time.

# SAMPLE CLASS
## ADVANCED LEVEL

One should take it for granted that when dancers reached this level of the Floor Barre studies they have learnt the entire vocabulary of the essential Warm-up and the Floor Barre exercises, so there is no more need to practise any movement with the support of a wall. Therefore, the exercises below are not new additions; they are already short *enchaînements,* chains of at least three or four combined exercises.

When the dancers have memorised and done these short chains of movements—in order to shorten the duration of the Warm-up section and also to enhance the dancers' stamina in the Floor Barre section—they should practise these combined *enchaînements* and merge them with others in an even longer chain, and so on. Exercising in this manner, the final sequence of movements should contain at least ten or more basic exercises. Evidently, they will have a relatively long duration, however, by exercising the body in long sequences—instead of interrupting the continuous flow of movements with frequent pauses—means gaining precious working-time during each lesson as well as raising the student's stamina. Also, body-heat can be raised in a short time, and then kept at a high level—which is the most essential prevention against injury.

Therefore, in the sample class described below the exercises (containing movement elements of a short chain) are grouped in such a way that in both the Warm-up and the Floor Barre sections at least two or three (later even more) of the following short chain of movement sequences can be bound together easily (for example exercises **a**, **b** and **c**, etc.). Naturally, executing these specifically long, combined and linked *enchaînements* is only possible when the dancers have lessons regularly for a certain period.

At advanced lessons all versions of previously learnt and practised exercises at beginners and intermediate levels should alternate. As the possibilities of combining and linking the movement elements belonging to the Warm-up and the Floor Barre section become endless, as well as dependent on the specific circumstance, individual need and personal capability, the following descriptions below are meant to serve as mere suggestions. However, it is hoped that the idea of how to build-up a class at an advanced level and the order of how the movement elements are grouped into the various *enchaînements* within a lesson will be followed so as to achieve the best results as far as injury prevention, rehabilitation after various illnesses and correcting faults is concerned.

# WARM-UP section

## Ankles, toes, knees & spine

a) **6/8. Lying on the back** with the legs in the 6<sup>th</sup> position and arms in a low diagonal. On the up-beat lift the bent right leg off the floor while holding the right thigh with both hands and pull it as close as possible towards the ribcage (and). Point the right foot while flexing the left (one-two-three) change feet positions (four-five-six); repeat this three more times; circle both feet *en dehors* (one-two-three-four-five-six); repeat the circles three more times and on the last count change the leg position; repeat the whole exercise with the left leg lifted to the chest. Perform the entire *enchaînement* again but this time lift the head and shoulders off the floor while the feet are pointing and flexing; then rest the head on the floor while the feet execute circles *en dedans* and *en dehors*. Finish the exercise by placing the left leg into the 6<sup>th</sup> position.

**Note:** At a somewhat later time of the studies—in order to be able to bind together this *enchaînement* with the following one—on the last count of this exercise leave the left leg in the bent position in the air and join it with the right leg also bent in a parallel position while holding onto both upper-legs with the hands.

b) **6/8.** Lying on the back with the legs in the 6<sup>th</sup> position. On the up-beat lift both legs off the floor bent while holding the upper-legs with the hands and pull them over the chest (and). Flex both feet while curling the toes under ('parrot's claws') and at the same time turn feet towards each other from the ankle ('sickle' inwards one-two-three); arch both feet and curl the toes upwards while turning the feet from the ankle away from each other ('sickle' out-wards four-five-six); repeat these movements three more times; while lifting the head and the shoulders off the floor stretch both leg upwards (one-two-three); drop both lower legs down keeping the feet relaxed (four-five-six); while keeping the head and shoulders lifted repeat the stretching and bending of the legs three more times but on the last beat of the exercise place them back onto the floor;

## Knees, hip joints & spine

c) **6/8.** Lying on the back  While holding the upper-legs with the hands circle the lower legs *en dehors* (one-two-three-four-five-six); reverse it *en dedans* (one-two-three-four-five-six); repeat everything three more times but on the last beat place both legs and arms stretched on the floor into 2<sup>nd</sup> position turning palms towards the floor; *passé* with the right leg turned out and with pointed foot (one-two-three-four-five-six); keep the right knee bent and turn in the leg while sliding the right leg on its inner side on the floor until the right upper-leg becomes parallel to the left upper-leg (one-two-three-four-five-six); repeat the turning out as well as the turning in of the bent leg three more times; perform the exercise four times with the left leg but when turning the left leg out for the fourth time bend the right leg also in a turned out *passé* position and, instead of turning in the left leg, just lift both bent legs into a parallel position with the feet placed flat on the floor; raise the pelvis into the air until the torso is in a perfectly straight diagonal line from the shoulders to the knees while raising the lower arms (placing the fingers lightly on the shoulders) and also the metatarsals off the floor three times (one-two, three-four, five-six); lower the pelvis and the lower arm onto the floor while lifting all the toes and the head in the air (one-two-three-four-five-six); repeat this exercise three more times.

**Note:** After a few lessons when the dancers have memorised exercises **a**, **b** and **c** separately, they should execute them one after the other as one long *enchaînement*.

## Knees, hip joints, ankles, spine, elbows & neck

d)   **4/4. Lying on the back** with the legs in the 1$^{st}$ position with flexed feet while the arms are in the 2$^{nd}$ position. *Passé* with the right leg with pointed foot (one-and); lift the bent leg and start turning it inwards while both lower arms are also lifted off the floor and start moving them in an *en dedans* circle (two-and); with the left hand grasp the turned-in right upper-leg and by allowing the pelvis to turn towards the left pull the bent right leg across to the left placing the right knee on the floor while the right lower-arm is finishing its *en dedans* circle (three-and); pull with the stretched right arm in 2$^{nd}$ position towards the right keeping both shoulders on the floor and turn the head to the right while pulling with the left arm the right leg even further across to the left (four-and); place the left arm into the 2$^{nd}$ position while letting the left leg go and placing the pelvis slowly back on the floor (one-and); continue moving the bent right leg *en dehors* while the lower arms start to move slowly in an *en dehors* circle (two-and); place the right leg onto the floor into a *passé* position while placing the arms into a 2$^{nd}$ position (three-and); stretch right leg into the 2$^{nd}$ position (four-and); repeat the whole procedure (one-and-two-and-three-and-four-and); do the first part of the exercise (the *en dedans* circling) at double speed (one-and-two-and); stretch the right leg across the left into a 90° *développé* position (three-and-four-and); flex the right foot (one-and-two-and); point the right foot (three-and-four-and); flex the right foot and hold it in this position (one-and-two-and-three-and-four-and); while the right leg is kept in the same position place the arms in the 5$^{th}$ position and slowly roll the body through the left side on to the tummy (one-and-two-and-three-and); close the right leg stretched into the 1$^{st}$ position with flexed feet while bending the elbows, place palms on the floor next to the shoulders (four-and);

push the ribcage off the floor into a vertical position while stretching the elbows (one-and); hold this position while turning the head to the right (two-and); turn the head to the left (three-and); turn head to the right (four-and); repeat the head movements to the left and right (one-and-two-and); place the ribcage onto the floor and rest (three-and-four-and); push the ribcage off the floor (one-and); execute a slow circle with the head (two-and-three-and-four-and) repeat the circle with the head (one-and-two-and-three-and-four-and); place the chest back onto the floor while sliding the hands forward into 5$^{th}$ position (one-and); raise the right leg into a *passé* position (two-and);  stretch the right leg on the floor with a flexed foot into a 90° *à la seconde* (three-and); roll on to the left side while keeping the right leg in the same position with the foot on the floor (four-and); continue rolling onto the back while bending the right leg into a *passé* in the 6$^{th}$ position and pointing the right foot (one-and);turn out both legs and place the *passé* onto the floor (two-and);while placing the right leg into the 2$^{nd}$ position bring the arms into the 2$^{nd}$ position and rest (three-and four-and). Execute the whole *enchaînement* to the other side starting with the left leg.

# Spine, neck & shoulders

**e) 4/4. Kneeling on all fours.** Keeping the hands on the floor drop the head forward while curving the spine upwards and sit back on the heels (one-and-two-and); lift the head and drop it backwards, start arching the back while bending the elbows and lower the ribcage, push the torso forward (three-and-four-and); repeat these curving and arching exercises three more times finishing the last movement on all fours with a straight spine; swing the pelvis to the right while dropping the head towards the right shoulder without turning it (one-and); do it to the other side (two-and); swing the pelvis three more times to the right and left with the above described head movements; sit back on the heels and stretch arms while resting the chest on the thighs (one-and-two-and-three-and-four-and); raise the bottom off the heels while sliding forward on the palms lowering the chest towards the floor (one-and-two-and-three-and-four-and); gradually stretch the knees until the whole body is lying comfortably on the stomach with the legs in a $1^{st}$ and the arms in a $5^{th}$ position (one-and-two-and-three-and-four-and); roll over to the back (one-and-two-and);

sit up in a wide $2^{nd}$ position while bending the arms and place fingers lightly on the shoulders (three-and-four-and); from the shoulders circle the arms once *en dehors* (one-and-and two-and); circle *en dedans* (three-and-four-and); again *en dehors* (one-and-two-and); again *en dedans* (three-and-four); open arms into a $2^{nd}$ position with the palms turned towards the floor (and); turn the top to the right by twisting the middle of the spine and the head follows the right arm reaching to the back across in a diagonal (one-and-two-and); twist and turn to the left (three-and-four-and); turn again to the right (one-and-two-and); turn to the left (three-and-four-and): turning again towards the right leave the head facing forward while bending and turning in the left leg to create a $4^{th}$ *arabesque* position and hold this, (one-and-two-and-three-and-four-and; one-and-two-and); turn the top of the torso *en face* while stretching the left knee into the wide $2^{nd}$ position (three-and-four-and); do the same to the left side (one-and-two-and-three-and-four-and).

**Note:** Once the dancers have memorised exercises **d** and **e** they can easily bind the two *enchaînements* together so that after the execution to both sides in exercise **d** on the last bar of the *enchaînement* just keep lying on the stomach (instead of turning from the stomach again on to the back) and by bending both knees push the whole torso into a 'kneeling on all fours' posture (four-and). Now exercise **e** can smoothly follow exercise **d.**

# FLOOR BARRE section

## Battement tendu combined with *passé* and *plié*

1. **4/4. Lying on the back** in the 6th position with the feet flexed and the arms either in the 5th position or with the hands placed below the nape of the neck. *Battement tendu en avant* with the right leg (one-and-two); close into the 6th position flexed (and); repeat the movement (three-and-four-and); *tendu* with flexed foot (one-and); point the right foot (two); flex it (and); point it (three); flex it (and); while turning out the left leg place the right leg flexed into the 1st position and raise the head, shoulders and the arms in 2nd position off the floor (four-and); while keeping the head, shoulders and arms *en l'air* repeat the *enchaînement* from the 1st position and on the last beat place the lifted top on the floor; execute the entire *enchaînement* with the left leg in such a way that at the end of it both legs close in a 6th position while placing the head, shoulders and arms on the floor;

   pull up the right leg into a *passé* with pointed foot (one-and-two); place it back to the 6th position (and); repeat with the right leg the *passé* and closing in the same rhythm (three-and-four-and); execute with both legs a slow *grand plié* in 6th position (one-and-two-and-three-and-four); finish it in the 1st position while lifting the head, shoulders and arms in the 2nd position off the floor (and); keeping the top of the torso in the air execute the turned-out *passé* with the right leg (one-and-two); close to 1st position (and); repeat the *passé* in the 1st position in the same rhythm; execute with both legs a *grand plié* (one-and-two-and-three-and-four); on the last count place legs into the 6th position and rest the head, shoulders and arms on the floor (and); execute the *passés* with the left leg and the *grand plié* in the 6th position with the torso resting on the floor; then lifting the head, shoulders and the arms in the 2nd position *en l'air* execute the *passés* with the left leg turned out in the 1st position followed by the *grand plié* in the 1st position and on the last beat place the lifted top on the floor.

   Now add a 'coda' to this *enchaînement* by doing eight fast, turned-out and evenly timed *battements tendus* to the side working with both legs at the same time followed by another eight *tendus* executed from the 6th position to the parallel position with flexed feet while lifting the head, shoulders and arms in the 2nd position in the air. On the last beat place the upper torso back onto the floor with relaxed neck and shoulders.

2. **4/4. Lying on the stomach,** the legs in 6th position with pointed feet while arms are either in the 'pentagon' position or the forehead rests on the hands. Execute all the *tendus* exactly the same way as performed in exercise 1 (including the lifting of the head, shoulders and arms) but, as it is impossible to do *passés* in the 6th position in this posture, all the *passés* in this *enchaînement* must be performed from a turned-out 1st position as well as the *grand pliés* in the 2nd position.

**Note:** Later link exercise **1** with exercise **2** in such a way that on the end of exercise 1 roll quickly onto the stomach and then continue executing exercise **2**.

## Demi-rond de jambe (par terre and en l'air) combined with attitude and fouetté

**3.**   **3/4. Lying on the back** with the legs in the 1ˢᵗ position while arms are in the low diagonal with the palms turned towards the floor. Two *demi-ronds des jambes en dehors* with the right leg (one-and-two-and-three-and; one-and-two-and-three) on the last count close the right leg into 5ᵗʰ position in front (and); perform three fast *demi-rond de jambe en dehors* (one-and; two-and; three-and); place the right leg into a *petite attitude* in the 4ᵗʰ position (one-and); stretch right leg and circle it *en dehors* into the 2ⁿᵈ position (two-and); close the right leg into the 1ˢᵗ position (three-and); repeat the whole *enchaînement* in such a way that whilst performing the *demi-ronds des jambes* the head, shoulders and arms in 2ⁿᵈ position are lifted up and then placed back onto the floor before the right leg starts to do the *attitude*. Also, this time the *attitude* should be lifted 90° high and the circling of the right leg finishes in a 90° *à la seconde*. Execute the whole *enchaînement* with the left leg.

**4.**   **3/4. Lying on the back** with the legs in the 1ˢᵗ position while the arms are resting on the floor in a low diagonal. Lift the right leg in an *en avant attitude* and at the same time sit up carrying the arms in a 5ᵗʰ position and turning the top an eighth towards the right (one-and-two-and-three-and); hold this position while turning the top slowly *en face* and opening the arms into 2ⁿᵈ position (one-and-two-ad-three-and); stretch the right leg in the air and start slowly curving the spine lowering the torso (one-and-two-and three-and); gradually lie back onto the floor with the arms in the 5ᵗʰ position whilst keeping the right leg in the air (one-and-two-and-three-and);

roll on to the left side placing the head onto the left arm while placing the right hand on the floor before the chest and holding the right leg straight in the *a la seconde* (one-and-two-and-three-and); roll on to the stomach while placing both hands next to the shoulders and bending the right leg into an *attitude derrière* (one-and-two-and-three-and); push the top off the floor into a 'sphinx' position (one-and-two-and-three-and); hold this position whilst lifting the left arm (or both arms) off the floor into a 5ᵗʰ position (one-and-two-and-three-and); roll on to the left side with the right hand placed on the floor in front of the chest while stretching the right leg and hold it in a 90° *à la seconde* position (one-and-two-and-three-and); roll on to the back while holding the right leg in a front *attitude* position at 90° and place both arms in a 2ⁿᵈ position (one-and-two-and-three-and); stretch the right leg and slowly place it on the floor in a 1ˢᵗ position and the arms into a low diagonal (one-and-two-and-three-and). Perform the whole *enchaînement* with the left leg.

**5.**   **3/4.** Perform exercise 3 in the **lying on the stomach** position.

**Note:** After practising this and exercise **4**, it is necessary to relieve the spine from the possible strain that the 'arching' movements might have caused. Therefore, it is important to counterbalance these with exercises designed to stretch the muscles of the centre spine in the opposite direction. (For example: see the **Mobilising the Spine** section, exercises **40** or **41**). When the dancers have learnt exercises **3**, **4** and **5** separately, they should link and practise them as one long *enchaînement* without a break.

## Battement fondus, développé with rond de jambe

6.  **4/4. Lying on the back** with the legs in 5th position while the arms are either bent with the palms beneath the nape of the neck or in a 2nd with palms turned towards the floor. On the up-beat open the right leg to the side with pointed foot. While placing the right foot pointed in front in a *coup de pied* position bend the left knee with the foot flexed (one-and-two-and); stretch the right leg to the front while stretching the left knee (three-and-four-and); perform now a *battement fondu* to the *à la seconde* (one-and-two-and-three-and-four-and); draw inwards the right leg into a 5th position (one-and); execute a slow *passé* with the right leg (two-and); stretch the leg in front to 90° high (or more) with flexed foot (three-and-four-and); turn in the stretched leg while pointing the foot (one-and); turn out the leg while pointing the foot (two-and); slowly place the right leg into the 5th position with flexed foot (four-and); now do one *battement fondu* to the side in double time (one-and); do one to the front (two-and); again to the side (three-and); again to the front (four-and); *développé* to the side with flexed foot into 90° (or higher) (one-and-two-and-three-and-four-and); turn the leg in while pointing the foot (one-and); turn the leg out (two-and); while placing the arms into the 5th position close the right leg also into the 1st position. Do the whole *enchaînement* with the left leg.

7.  **Lying on the left side** in 1st position pointing with both feet while the head rests on the stretched left arm and the right hand is placed onto the floor in front of the chest. On the upbeat open the right leg with pointed foot to the side at 45° (and-), move the right leg and foot like a 'paint-brush' by flexing the right foot while drawing the leg into the front of the left ankle with a soft quality (one-and); while pointing the right foot stretch the right leg smoothly to the side (two-and); repeat this movement three more times stretching the leg always to the side but alternating the withdrawal of the right leg to the back, then to the front and again to the back (two-and, three-and, four-and); *passé* with the right leg (one-and); stretch the right leg into a 90° angle (or higher) with a flexed foot (two-and); point the right foot while turning in the leg (three-and); flex the right foot while turning out the leg (four-and); single *rond de jambe en l'air en dehors* (one-and); single *rond de jambe en dedans* (two-and); *double ronds de jambes en l'air en dehors* (three-and); hold the leg in the *à la seconde* position stretched (four-and); starting it *en dedans* repeat this combination of *ronds des jambes* three more times in such a way that after the last *double ronds de jambes*, instead of holding the leg in the *à la seconde*, close it immediately in the 1st position and roll on to the right side (four-and). Perform the whole *enchaînement* with the left leg.

**Note:** When the dancers have practised and memorised this *enchaînement* as well as the previous one the two *enchaînements* should be linked together so that when exercise **6** finishes in the 1st position the dancer at the same time rolls on the left side and on the last beat places the right leg to the side (and).

8.  **4/4. Lying on the stomach** in the 5th position with the right leg in the back while the forehead rests on the hands. On the up-beat point the right foot placing it behind the left ankle (and). Perform four *battements fondus* to the *à la seconde* (each *battement fondu* lasting for four slow counts); execute four slow *battements fondus* to the back (each *battement fondu* lasting for four slow counts); pull the bent knee into a *passé* in the 1st position with pointed foot

(one-and-two-and); pull the left leg also into a *passé* with pointed foot whereby achieving a *grand plié* in the 1ˢᵗ position (one-and-two-and-three-and-four-and); execute an irregular *rond de jambe en dehors* with the right lower leg (one-and-two-and) (see exercise **122**, **Figures 109**, **110** and **111**); do another irregular *rond de jambe en dedans*, then again an *en dehors* and an *en dedans* one while with each circling movement raise the upper-leg gradually to a higher angle (three-and-four-and, one-and-two-and, three-and-four-and);

unfold the right leg into a *développé* to the *à la seconde* at 90° (one-and-two-and); flex the foot (three-and); point the foot while climbing with it at a slightly higher angle (four-and); flex it (one-and); point it and simultaneously climb a bit higher again (two-and); flex it (three-and); point and climb a fraction higher (four-and); place both arms into the 5ᵗʰ position whilst stretching the left leg into the starting 1ˢᵗ position and bend the top to the right sideways above the right leg (one-and-two-and-three-and-four-and); slowly recover the spine to its original straight line (one-and-two-and-three-and-four-and); slowly withdraw the right leg to the 1ˢᵗ position (one-and-two-and-three-and-four-and). Perform the whole *enchainement* to the left.

**Note:** After exercise **8** is practised and memorised it should be linked with the already combined exercises **6** and **7** in such a way that when exercise **7** is executed to the second side on the last beat the dancer should roll on to the stomach.

## Adage

9.  **4/4. Lying on the back** with the legs in the 6ᵗʰ position with the feet pointed and hands below the nape of the neck. *Passé* with the right leg (one-and-two-and); stretch the right leg to the front into a 90° angle (three-and-four-and); turn out both legs and flex the feet (one-and-two-and); while leaving the left leg turned out and with the foot flexed on the floor, turn in the right leg with pointed foot (three-and-four-and); turn out the right leg (one-and); turn in the right leg (two-and); turn out the right leg and with pointed foot place it into an *attitude en avant* position (three-and-four-and); lift the head and shoulders off the floor stretch the arms slowly into the 2ⁿᵈ position while stretching the right leg and with a circling movement place it *à la seconde* (or just above it) on the floor with flexed foot at 90° (one-and-two-and-three-and-four-and); while placing the top on the floor turn in the right leg with pointed foot (one-and); turn it out and flex the foot (two-and); turn it in with pointed foot (three-and); turn out with flexed foot (four-and);

withdraw the pointed foot into a *passé retiré* (one-and-two-and); place the right leg with flexed foot into a 1ˢᵗ position (three-and-four-and); while raising the head, shoulders and arms in the air lift the right leg with pointed foot and perform a slow *grand rond de jambe en dehors* (one-and-two-and-three-and); when the right leg is closing the 1ˢᵗ position with flexed foot place the top of the torso simultaneously on the floor (four-and); execute with the right leg a *grand rond de jambe en dedans* while lifting again the head, shoulders and arms off the floor (one-and-two-and-three-and); close the 1ˢᵗ position with flexed foot while lowering the top to the floor (four-and). Perform the whole *enchaînement* with the left leg.

**10. 4/4. Lying on the back** with the legs in the 1st or 5th position with the feet flexed whilst the arms are in a 5th. Lift the right leg in front with pointed foot to 90° (one-and-two-and); with a circular movement place it to the *à la seconde* (three-and-four and); flex the right foot (one); point it and at the same time push the right leg a fraction further up (and); repeat the flexing and pointing actions three more times always pushing the leg and pointing the foot further upwards (two-and-three-and-four-and); roll on to the left side resting the head on the left arm while turning the right leg into an *arabesque* position trying to touch the floor with the right big toe (one-and-two-and-three-and-four-and); place the right arm stretched in the air in front—as in a 2nd *arabesque*—while the left leg on the floor pushes forward into the 'splits' with pointed foot (one-and-two-and-three-and-four-and);

lift the right arm into the 5th position while bending the right leg into an *attitude* position (one-and-two-and); stretch the right knee again into an *arabesque* while the left leg on the floor pushes a bit further, while the right arm is placed again forwards (three-and-four-and); placing the arms into 5th position, roll on to the back trying to keep the legs at the same angle as in the previous 'split' *arabesque* but now in the *à la seconde* position (one-and-two-and); keeping the legs in this position flex both feet (three); point the feet (and) flex them (four); point them (and); slowly control the lowering of the right leg until it reaches the 2nd position (one-and-two-and-three-and); close both legs into a 1st position with flexed feet (four-and). Perform the whole *enchaînement* to the left.

**Note:** When the dancers have practised and memorised exercises **9** and **10** they should link them together and execute them without a break.

**11. 4/4. Lying on the back** with flexed feet the legs are in 1st position, while the arms are resting on the floor next to the torso. Start performing with the right leg a *grand rond de jambe en dedans* through a *battement tendu* to the side, move the right leg just above the floor to the *à la seconde* 90° while placing the arms to the 2nd position and raising the head and shoulders off the floor (one-and-two-and); lift the right leg and carry it into an *attitude en avant* position at 90° and at the same time carry the arms into a 5th position and lower head and shoulders to the floor (three-and-four-and); roll on to the left side and whilst stretching the right leg into an *à la seconde* at 90° place the right hand onto the floor in the front of the chest (one-and-two-and); move the right leg into an *en avant attitude* with a circular movement (three-and-four and); lowering the big toe of the right foot on to the floor, slowly roll on to the stomach moving the right arm into the 5th position and while stretching the knee place the right leg on the floor into an *à la seconde* position (one-and-two-and); point the right foot while pushing the right leg to a somewhat higher angle than 90° (three); flex the foot (and); point it and raise the leg a bit further (four); flex it again (and);

roll on to the left side and place the right hand on the floor in front of the chest and, while pointing both feet, bend the right knee into an *attitude en avant* position (one-and-two-and); while stretching the right leg carry it to the *à la seconde* (three-and-four-and); continue the *en dehors grand rond de jambe* with the right leg into an *attitude* position *en arrier* (one-and-two-and); stretch the leg into *arabesque* and at the same time lift the right hand off the floor and stretch the right arm also into an *arabesque* position (three-and-four-and); bend the right knee into *attitude* while pushing the left leg a bit more forwards ('split') while carrying the right arm into 5th position (one-and-two-and-); perform a 'split' *arabesque* (three-and-four-and); while keeping the left leg on the floor at the same angle flex the left foot and roll on to the back while arms are in the 5th position and the right leg stretches into an *à la seconde* with flexed foot (one-and-two-and); point the feet whilst pushing both legs a little more apart from each other (three-and); flex both feet (four-and); keeping both feet flexed carry slowly the legs into the 1st position (one-and-two-and); rest (three-and-four-and). Perform the whole *enchaînement* with the left leg to the other side.

**Note:** When the dancers have practised and memorised this *enchaînement* it should be linked together with exercises **9** and **10**.

## Grand battement with *petit battement, battement frappé* and *entrechat six*

12. **6/8. Lying on the left side** in a 1st position with the feet pointed whilst the head is resting on the stretched left arm and the right hand is placed on the floor in front of the chest. On the up-beat execute a *battement tendu* to the *à la seconde* as a preparation (and). Execute to the side two *double frappés* (one-two-three, four-five-six); perform twelve *petits battements* alternating front to back (one-two-three-four-five-six, one-two-three-four-five-six); *grand battement* to the *à la seconde* with flexed foot (one-two-three); close the 1st position with pointed foot (four-five-six); repeat the *grand battement* (one-two-three-four-five-six); repeat the *enchaînement* three more times in such a way that while the dancer swings the right leg to the last *grand battement à la seconde* she/he rolls on to the back while the leg is turned *en dehors* to the front (one-two-three); close the right leg into the 1st position with both feet pointed and roll on to the right side (four-five-six). Perform the whole *enchaînement* now with the left leg whilst lying on the right side. With the last *grand battement* roll on to the back.

13. **6/8. Lying on the back** with the legs in 6th position, feet flexed and the arms in the 2nd position with palms turned towards the floor. Do one *grand battement* to the front with pointed foot (one-two-three, four-five-six) repeat this but finish it in a 5th position (one-two-three, four-five-six); now perform the same from the 5th position and finish it in the 6th position while raising the head, shoulders and arms off the floor: place head and shoulders back to the floor while executing two more *grands battements* finishing the last one in a 5th position; while lifting the head, shoulders and arms again lift both legs just above the floor and do an *entrechat royale* (or *six)* and place the legs on the floor in 5th position with flexed feet, left leg in front (one-two-three-four-five-six); lift legs again and execute an *entrechat six* and on the last beat place the legs as well as the head and shoulders on the floor (one-two-three-four-five-six); repeat the whole *enchaînement* so that instead of the last *entrechat six* do only an *entrechat quatre.* Having now the left leg in front perform the whole lot to the other side.

**Note:** When the dancers have practised and memorised this exercise they should link and practise *enchaînements* **12** and **13** without a break in between them.